passageway, each with one forward-facing arrowloop and two further loops opening into the gate-passage.

Carrying on right around the rear of the gatehouse [11], the modern timber steps lead up to first-floor level. Here, in a single great room, it was necessary to accommodate the controls for the two portcullises used to block the gate-passage below. Otherwise, it appears to have been a fine and comfortable apartment which probably served as the lord's personal hall. It was equipped with a large fireplace and flanking windows in the south wall, and there were four arrowloops covering the gatehouse front.

At the far end of this chamber, a spiral stair winds up past latrines to the roof. A break in the side wall leads through to what is now a platform above the Tudor gateway. The upper storey of the gatehouse (its floor now missing) housed another well-appointed and large chamber, which is likely to have been a private stateroom, or solar. It was again fitted with a grand fireplace between two tall windows. The window to the left (east), later blocked, retains fragments of its tracery; these are best viewed from outside.

Having returned to ground level, walk past the badly damaged west tower [12] and enter the upper ward through the inner gate [13]. This small, square tower is of early thirteenth-century date and has a plain pointed gate arch. The entry was defended by a portcullis (of which a groove remains), and by doors secured with stout wooden bars. There is a single room on each of the two upper floors. The roof and battlements can only have been reached by means of a ladder and a trapdoor from the second-floor room.

The stone curtain wall, which formerly adjoined the inner gate and bounded the upper ward, has now vanished. But it incorporated a strong circular tower whose foundations remain [14]. The other foundations in this area are of a later medieval date, though it is difficult to be certain of their use. One of the rectangular chambers [15] was approached down a flight of steps from the upper ward; it was equipped with a fireplace in its east wall.

Elsewhere in the upper ward you should note the castle well [16], and the arched vaults situated against the north-western section of the curtain wall [17]. These vaults were added during the later thirteenth century, in a phase of construction when the earlier wall was

Top: The back of the later thirteenth-century great gatehouse. The small drum towers contained spiral stairs, giving access to the upper floors from the first floor.

Above left: Two large chambers, extending the full width of the gatehouse, occupied the first and second floors. Both were equipped with large fireplaces; that on the upper floor, shown here, was particularly fine.

Above right: The inner gate protected the entrance into the upper ward. Traces of the late twelfth-century curtain wall can be seen in its lower courses.

strengthened and raised in height. Their main purpose was to provide an arcade to support a new and sufficiently wide wall-walk.

You should now return to the lower ward and look at the details of the north tower [4]. It was of three storeys and was probably designed to house the castle's other principal domestic accommodation. The upper floors were accessed via a stair turret. In each of the upper chambers there was a fireplace and two windows.

Nearby, the defensive east bastion [6] looks like a corner tower, but in fact it is no more than a great clasping buttress strengthening this corner of the castle.

The gable-ended building [18] between the north tower and the bastion is a Tudor barn. It may have replaced the hall-block of the thirteenth-century castle.

Further Reading

R. R. Davies, *Conquest, Coexistence, and Change: Wales 1063–1415* (Oxford 1987); reprinted in paperback as *The Age of Conquest: Wales 1063–1415* (Oxford 1991).

G. C. Guilbert and J. J. Schweiso, 'Llanstephan Castle: An Interim Discussion of the 1971 Excavation', *Carmarthenshire Antiquary* 8 (1972), 75–90.

G. C. Guilbert, 'Llanstephan Castle: 1973 Interim Report', *Carmarthenshire Antiquary* 10 (1974), 37–48.

D. J. C. King, *Llanstephan Castle* (HMSO, London 1963).

Richard Avent, 'The Early Development of Three Coastal Castles', in H. James, editor, *Sir Gâr: Studies in Carmarthenshire History* (Carmarthen 1991), pp. 167–88.

Tour of the Castle

The hilltop can only be approached on foot, and visitors should follow the signs to the castle from Llansteffan village and the car parks along the foreshore. A pathway leads up to the headland, where the climb is rewarded with superb views of the estuary and the surrounding countryside.

At the top of the path, before entering the castle, several external features may be noticed. In the field on the right (which is private property) are [1] the outer defensive bank and ditch of the medieval castle and, further to the right [2], the slighter banks and ditches of the much earlier Iron Age promontory fort. In front of you is the imposing twin-towered gatehouse of the late thirteenth century [3]. The gate-passage between the towers was

blocked up at the end of the fifteenth century, but the outline of the original archway is still plainly visible. Above the arch, note the remains of a sloping chute through which water could be poured to douse any fire set against the gate.

Walking on to the head of the rise, one can appreciate how the large, projecting north tower [4] dominates the defences on the landward side. You may wish to follow the grass path down past this tower, noting its latrine outlet [5], and on as far as the corner east bastion [6], before retracing your steps to enter the lower ward. The later and relatively weakly defended entrance through which you pass was inserted during the early Tudor period [7]. There was a single undistinguished chamber above this entrance.

Once inside the lower ward, turn to your right and look at the back of the great gatehouse. The small corner drum towers contained spiral staircases that gave access from the first floor to the upper levels. At ground level, there is a small doorway [8] located in the masonry blocking of a much larger opening. This blocked-up opening represents the inner end of the thirteenth-century gate-passage. Inside the vaulted gate-passage [9], various features of the original arrangement can still be seen: in the roof are grooves — front and rear — in which the portcullises once slid, and there are two series of five murder holes through which projectiles might be dropped on an unwelcome raiding party. Guard-chambers [10] are situated in the D-shaped towers to either side of the

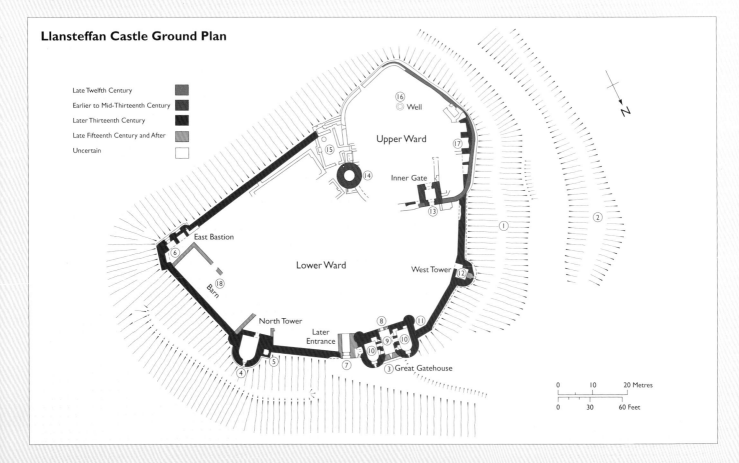

Llansteffan Castle Ground Plan

Late Twelfth Century
Earlier to Mid-Thirteenth Century
Later Thirteenth Century
Late Fifteenth Century and After
Uncertain

Well 16
Upper Ward
17
15
14
Inner Gate
13
East Bastion
6
1
2
18
Lower Ward
West Tower 12
Barn
North Tower
8 11
Later Entrance
9 10
10
7
4
5
3 Great Gatehouse

N

0   10   20 Metres
0   30   60 Feet

pre-eminent in many parts of the country, his hold soon waned in the south-west, where William Marshal the younger (d. 1231) succeeded in recovering Cardigan and Carmarthen in 1223. He probably restored Llansteffan to the Camvilles at this time also. Improvements to the defences of the upper ward were now carried out, including the addition of the still prominent square gatehouse tower and the round mural tower, whose foundations can be seen in the upper ward.

Further tribulation was to follow in June 1257, when the Welsh inflicted a devastating defeat at Coed Llathen on an English army attempting to march from Carmarthen to Dinefwr Castle. The army was apparently composed of men drawn from the garrisons of English castles in the region, which were thus left defenceless in the face of follow-up action by the Welsh. Yet again, Llansteffan was one of the first to be taken, but Carmarthen held out and the Welsh success was short-lived. Returning to a castle somewhat damaged by this affair, William de Camville II probably began a programme of modernization during the 1260s, which gave the castle its present form. The timber defences of the lower ward were replaced by a powerful stone curtain wall with strong mural towers and, at the same time, it is clear that the curtain wall of the upper ward was also heightened and strengthened.

As a continuation of this phase, the great outer gatehouse was added to the lower ward. It resembles the inner east gatehouse at Caerphilly Castle (which dates from about 1270), but its features appear to predate those of the great gatehouses of King Edward I's north Wales castles of the 1280s. It seems likely, therefore, that the Llansteffan gate was built during the time of William's successor, Geoffrey de Camville II (d. 1309), who became lord about 1275.

The male line of the Camvilles ended with the death of William III in 1338, and Llansteffan passed through marriage to the Penres family from Gower. The castle was to see a further brief spell of action during the revolt of Owain Glyn Dŵr, when it was in Welsh hands for a period in 1405–06, but it is not clear whether it was at this time that the curtain wall and mural tower between the two wards were breached, and later dismantled.

For the next two centuries, Llansteffan was held chiefly by the Crown, though it was

Above: Prince Rhys ap Gruffudd of Deheubarth (d. 1197), better known as the Lord Rhys, succeeded in capturing Llansteffan Castle twice. His tomb effigy lies in St Davids Cathedral.

Above: The Camville arms on a seal of William de Camville, appended to an early thirteenth-century grant of lands in the vicinity of Llansteffan Castle (The National Archives/PRO, E 210/8314).

A general view across the upper ward of Llansteffan Castle, which occupies the same position as the earthwork castle raised soon after 1100. The foundations of the round mural tower can be seen in the foreground, with the inner gatehouse beyond. Both date from the earlier part of the thirteenth century when the castle was further fortified in stone, following its recovery from the Welsh.

repeatedly granted away. At the end of the fifteenth century, King Henry VII (1485–1509) conferred the castle on his uncle, Jasper Tudor (d. 1495), and it was perhaps at this time that modifications were made to the castle entrance. The gatehouse passageway was blocked up to provide extra accommodation and a simple entrance was constructed alongside.

The military importance of the site had thus declined and Llansteffan was to pass into relative obscurity.

A long period of neglect ended in 1959 when the castle was placed in State care. It is now maintained by Cadw, the historic environment service of the Welsh Assembly Government.

Reconstructions of the Castle

It was probably in the 1260s that William de Camville II began a programme of major rebuilding at Llansteffan, and it seems likely that the work continued into the time of his son, Geoffrey II. These two illustrations give an impression of the results of this phase of construction.

The great gatehouse was undoubtedly influenced by the work of Gilbert de Clare (d. 1295) at Caerphilly, but preceded the more accomplished gatehouses of King Edward I in north Wales. The Llansteffan gate-passage was blocked in the late Middle Ages, and it is difficult to appreciate the original arrangements without an attempt at reconstruction.

William and Geoffrey de Camville left the castle with a very powerful stone ring of defences around the lower ward, which was entered by the new gatehouse. The much smaller curtain wall around the upper ward may have survived for a time, but it was soon to become redundant and was apparently dismantled.

These artist's impressions show how Llansteffan Castle may have looked in the late thirteenth century. The cutaway view of the great gatehouse (above) shows the gate-passage defended by two portcullises, two sets of double doors and murder holes. Note how, when the portcullises were raised, they would have intruded into the comfortable first-floor hall.

The overall view of the castle (left) shows the towers and defences of the two wards defended in stone. Ancillary buildings, such as stables and barns, are likely to have been built in timber on stone foundations. Note the prominence of the north tower in the foreground, which probably contained handsome apartments for the castle's lord (Illustrations by Garth Lloyd, 1987).

© Cadw, Welsh Assembly Government (Crown Copyright), Plas Carew, Cefn Coed, Parc Nantgarw, Cardiff CF15 7QQ. First Published 1988; Revised 1996; Third Edition 2006 ISBN 1 85760 233 1
Cover: Llansteffan Castle from the north-west with the Tywi estuary beyond (© Crown Copyright).

Cadw yw gwasanaeth amgylchedd hanesyddol Llywodraeth Cynulliad Cymru. Ei nod yw hyrwyddo gwaith cadwraeth ar gyfer amgylchedd hanesyddol Cymru a gwerthfawrogiad ohono.
www.cadw.cymru.gov.uk

Cadw is the Welsh Assembly Government's historic environment service. Its aim is to promote the conservation and appreciation of Wales's historic environment.
www.cadw.wales.gov.uk

ISBN 1-85760-233-1

9 781857 602333

Llansteffan Castle

Cadw

Llywodraeth Cynulliad Cymru
Welsh Assembly Government

History of the Castle

Peter H. Humphries AMA

The castle of Llansteffan stands in a wonderfully picturesque location, crowning the top of a well-defined headland looking out over the broad sand-flats of the Tywi estuary. This strong hilltop position was first fortified in the prehistoric Iron Age and by the sixth century BC a double bank and ditch had been thrown across the neck of the headland to create a defensive promontory fort.

It is hardly surprising, therefore, that the Norman invaders also recognized the defensive potential of the site. Like a number of Anglo-Norman strongholds similarly sited along the indented coastline of south Wales, Llansteffan was positioned to take full advantage of seaborne communication, which proved to be of critical importance during the frequently troubled years of the twelfth and thirteenth centuries. And, like its neighbours to the east and west at Kidwelly and Laugharne, the castle was sited to control a river crossing and to guard an exposed waterway, which gave access into the heart of the country.

Although we cannot say exactly when the castle was first established, it was probably raised by the Norman invaders during their initial penetration of south-west Wales, soon after 1100. The castle created at this time, within the prehistoric defences, was of a form known as a 'ringwork'. The defended area was enclosed by an earth bank, crowned by a timber palisade, with an outer ditch along the western side. These defences followed the line of the present upper ward, though archaeological excavations have revealed traces of what may have been a second ward of the early Norman stronghold.

But it is not until 1146 that we have the first definite reference to Llansteffan. In that year, the Welsh *Brut y Tywysogyon* (*Chronicle of the Princes*) records that the castle was taken by Maredudd ap Gruffudd (d. 1155) and his brothers, Cadell (d. 1175) and Rhys (d. 1197), young princes of the royal house of Deheubarth (south-west Wales). Shortly afterwards,

Llansteffan Castle from the north-east. The first castle, an earth-and-timber ringwork established soon after 1100, took advantage of the existing banks and ditches of an Iron Age promontory fort. The masonry defences were constructed in the late twelfth and thirteenth centuries. The gate-passage of the great twin-towered gatehouse was blocked during the early Tudor period to create further accommodation (RCAHMW).

Maredudd succeeded in repelling a much larger Norman force sent to recapture the castle, throwing them off their scaling ladders and into the ditch. By 1158, however, the district had been reoccupied by the Normans and the castle was generally in English hands thereafter.

From the end of the twelfth century, Llansteffan was held by William de Camville and his descendants (apparently five lords in all — alternately named William and Geoffrey). During this period the castle had something of a chequered history: it was three times captured by the Welsh, and three times retaken by the English. In 1189, the Lord Rhys (who had taken the castle with his brothers in 1146) launched an attack on several English-held territories in south-west Wales. Llansteffan was taken at once, but it was not

held for long, as William de Camville is recorded as being back in possession by 1192. William borrowed money to refortify the defences and it is likely that the earliest masonry in Llansteffan's upper ward dates from this period. The bank was revetted in stone and carried up as a low wall to provide basic protection, and a simple gateway was built to give access from the lower ward, which seems to have continued to rely on its timber defences.

The next Welsh attack came in 1215: seeing his English opponents embroiled in disagreement over Magna Carta, Llywelyn ab Iorwerth (d. 1240), prince of Gwynedd, promptly overran large areas of south Wales and captured many castles, Llansteffan amongst them. Although Llywelyn remained

VANISHING POINT

Perspective for Comics
From the Ground Up

Jason Cheeseman-Meyer

IMPACT
CINCINNATI, OHIO
www.impact-books.com

Other fine IMPACT Books are available from your local bookstore, art supply store or direct from the publisher at www.impact-books.com.

11 10 09 08 07   5 4 3 2 1

DISTRIBUTED IN CANADA BY FRASER DIRECT
100 Armstrong Avenue
Georgetown, ON, Canada L7G 5S4
Tel: (905) 877-4411

DISTRIBUTED IN THE U.K. AND EUROPE BY DAVID & CHARLES
Brunel House, Newton Abbot, Devon, TQ12 4PU, England
Tel: (+44) 1626 323200, Fax: (+44) 1626 323319
E-mail: postmaster@davidandcharles.co.uk

DISTRIBUTED IN AUSTRALIA BY CAPRICORN LINK
P.O. Box 704, S. Windsor NSW, 2756 Australia
Tel: (02) 4577-3555

Library of Congress Cataloging in Publication Data
Cheeseman-Meyer, Jason.
 Vanishing point : perspective for comics from the ground up / Jason Cheeseman-Meyer.
      p. cm.
 Includes bibliographical references and index.
 ISBN-13: 978-1-58180-954-1 (alk. paper)
 ISBN-10: 1-58180-954-9 (alk. paper)
 1. Perspective. 2. Drawing--Technique. 3. Cartooning--Technique. I. Title.
 NC750.C442 2008
 741.5'1--dc22
                          2007027254

Edited by Jacqueline Musser
Production edited by Sarah Laichas
Designed by Guy Kelly
Production coordinated by Matt Wagner

Metric Conversion Chart

To convert	to	multiply by
Inches	Centimeters	2.54
Centimeters	Inches	0.4
Feet	Centimeters	30.5
Centimeters	Feet	0.03
Yards	Meters	0.9
Meters	Yards	1.1

About the Author

Jason Cheeseman-Meyer is an artist, illustrator and writer currently living in Arizona with his wife and two daughters. Formally educated at Oberlin College after a stint at Otis College of Art and Design, he continues his arts education with artists and illustrators around the country. Jason has studied curvilinear perspective since 1993. He has utilized his background in art, math, teaching and, of course, comic books, in devising a practical system for drawing and teaching curvilinear perspective.

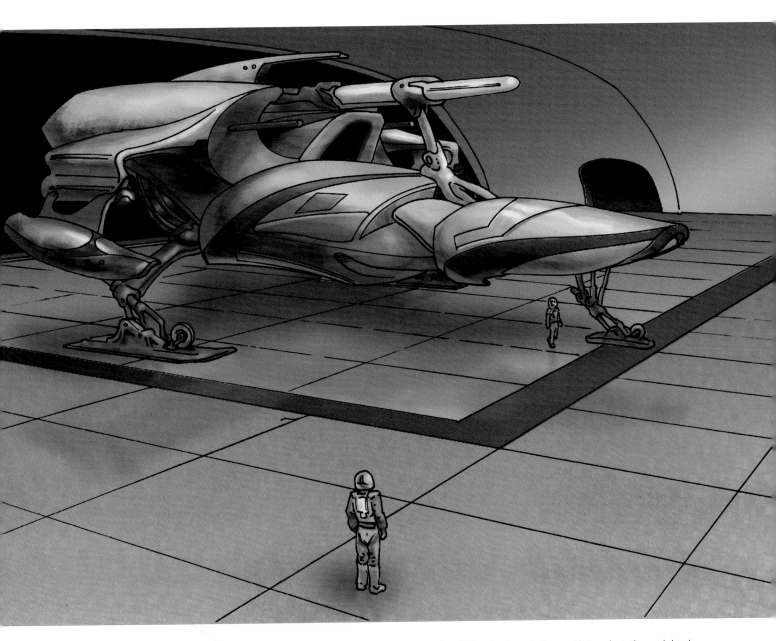

Acknowledgments

When I set out to write this book, I asked my fellow artists what they wished perspective books would cover, and found almost all of them were resentful about how many important concepts perspective books had never seen fit to share. Then I talked to friends and friends of friends to whom perspective drawing had never made any sense, to find ways to make the concepts instantly clear. It's my sincere hope that this book delivers to both of these groups, and thank you to everyone who talked with me.

I owe many people debts of gratitude on behalf of this book: Ellen made it physically possible for me to write this book; John F. was the first to tell me "you should make a book out of this," and his questions about perspective helped shape my teaching approach (not to mention he showed me a thing or two in the process); and Rush W. sparked my interest in the possibilities of perspective drawing—way back in 1993—into a fire that's never cooled down. I also owe a debt to Albert Flocon and André Barre, whose system of curvilinear perspective drawing helped fill the final holes in my own system.

To this I add the legions of artists past and present who have inspired me.

Contents

Introduction

Cities, people, trees, waterfalls, playing cards, cars: Everything you see, you see in perspective. In comic book and fantasy art you're drawing whole worlds, scenes from all angles, characters and objects in extreme foreshortening, all in perspective—you really need to know your stuff.

I've written this book to cover all the bases of perspective drawing. It even dives headlong into curvilinear perspective, where "straight" lines are drawn as curves. It's a powerful way to draw and gives us alternative views of the world, but it hasn't been taught in any of the major perspective books—until this one!

This book has to go further than other perspective books because comic book and fantasy art are generally based on invention rather than observation. We're inventing scenes from worlds no one else can see. The information we put on the pages comes from our minds rather than our eyes. Once our minds develop an intuitive understanding of perspective, we can work not only from observation to image, but from concept through construction to image—"from the ground up."

Vanishing Point is a dual-purpose text. Go through the chapters, follow the step-by-step demonstrations, draw, and your mind will begin developing that intuitive understanding of perspective. The lessons of each chapter are built upon in the following chapters. You'll quickly learn the nuts and bolts you need for 95 percent of your drawings.

This book also has a series of technical tricks for that remaining 5 percent, and they can get complicated. But "complicated" doesn't mean "advanced," or even "hard." These tricks actually make drawing easier by taking away the trial-and-error guesswork.

Many times perspective books (or perspective teachers) will tell you to "place the vanishing points," or "draw a

set of vertical lines," but not tell you where to do so. If you press them, you might get "in the right place," but how do you know where the right place is? "With experience, you'll just get a feel for where they should go," is a common answer. Well, that's true, but there are better answers out there. This book tries to collect the best of them, and breaks them down to help you draw as though you have decades more drawing experience than you actually do. There's no need for memorization—you've got this book as a reference manual that you can pull off the shelf any time you need to.

Supplies for perspective drawing are basic and readily available at your local art supply store. Purchase the best materials you can afford. Here's what you'll need:

Pencils

You can draw with any pencil that suits you. If you're going to ink the drawing, use a lead that's hard enough, light and easy to erase, but soft enough that it won't etch dents into the paper. I usually use an HB and a light touch.

Erasers

Different erasers are good for different things. A kneaded eraser softens things up. A harder, white eraser really eradicates things. It's a good idea to have both.

Triangles

Perspective drawings require a lot of right angles, so a triangle is a necessity. Triangles come in many sizes and shapes. A 45-degree triangle lets you measure 45-degree angles as well as 90-degree angles, but some people prefer using a 30/60/90 triangle.

Rulers/Straightedges

The straightedge is the most-used tool of straight-line perspective. It should be at least 18 inches (46cm) in length and trans-parent, making it easier to see if your line is placed correctly. Place small blocks of tape on the bottom to hold the ruler up off the drawing surface so the ink doesn't smear. (But avoid putting the tape squares down in a spot of wet ink.)

Lightbox

While not essential, the lightbox is a great tool. It allows you to trace images onto heavy paper. It lets you create construction drawings and underdrawings on one page, and the finished drawing on another, rather than having to erase all your construction lines. Lightboxes are available in various sizes and price ranges. As long as it's big enough to fit your finished-size paper, and strong enough to let you see through your finished paper, it's enough to do the job.

Technologically, the lightbox isn't a complicated machine—mine is homemade, white on the inside with an off-the-shelf fluorescent lamp in it. The drawing surface is frosted Plexiglas to diffuse the light and real glass on top for a durable surface. The result is much cheaper than any pre-made lightbox anywhere near this one's luxuri-ous size (28" × 20"; 71cm × 52cm). You want something big enough to fit 11" × 17" (28cm × 43cm) comic pages.

Pencils

Erasers

Hard, White Erasers

Kneaded Eraser

Triangles

Lightbox

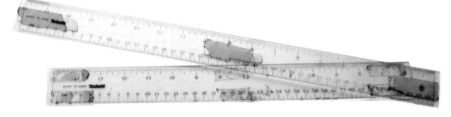

Rulers/Straightedges

Templates

Ellipse templates aren't essential, but they are handy when it comes time to draw circles in perspective. And sometimes a circle template is easier than using a compass to draw an actual circle.

Compass

The compass is the primary tool for drawing in curvilinear perspective. A good compass needs two things—the ability to draw big circles and, more importantly, the ability to be adjusted quickly. Curvilinear drawing requires constant fiddling with the compass settings. If you have to spin the adjusting wheel every time, it could get frustrating.

This compass pictured is fitted with a compass extension beam. (You might have to buy this beam separately, so make sure you get one that matches the make of your compass.) The extension beam lets you draw much larger circles than the compass alone. Also, it allows you to adjust the compass setting very quickly.

I also added a penholder adapter to my compass so I can draw circles in ink or with my favorite grade of pencil.

Beam Compass

A slightly nicer compass solution is the beam compass. They can be expensive, but you can sometimes find them secondhand for very low prices (this is true of many drafting tools). A beam compass is a long beam or bar with two feet that can slide along its length. They generally have a much longer reach than a standard compass (even a compass with an extension beam) and some of them are very fast to adjust.

A low-budget model is simply a pointer and a pencil foot that attach to a yardstick, ruler or paint stick. This is not as fast as some of the others, but it's a good value.

French Curve

A good French curve (or ship's curve) is particularly handy in curvilinear perspective drawing when a compass isn't practical. It's also great for straight-line perspective drawings of sleekly curving objects like cars and spaceships.

Flexible Curve

For times when a normal French curve doesn't have quite what you need, there are a number of adjustable flexible curves on the market. Flexible ship curves are harder to use (and to find) but create a beautiful, flowing sweep. Flexible curves can hardly be considered "required tools," but they're occasionally quite useful.

Templates

Compass

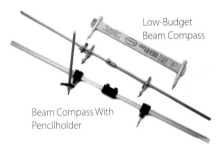
Beam Compasses

Low-Budget Beam Compass

Beam Compass With Pencilholder

French Curve

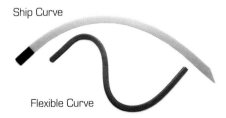
Ship Curve

Flexible Curve

Any Medium Will Do

The concepts of perspective drawing are the same no matter what medium you use. But if you're interested, the illustrations in this book were inked with sable brushes, Hunt 108 Flexible quills, and a Pentel Pocket Brush Pen, and were digitally colored.

CHAPTER ONE

WHAT IS PERSPECTIVE?

Before you can draw anything,

you need to learn how to draw with perspective. It doesn't matter what you're drawing: people, buildings, cars, landscapes, still lifes or whatever. If it exists in space, then it's affected by perspective.

The most basic concept of perspective is that things look smaller the farther away they are from the viewer. As objects like fence posts, train tracks or rows of rooftops grow smaller in the distance, they line up and point toward a single spot in the infinite distance. The tools of perspective exist in order to capture this convergence.

Comic book art and fantasy art can be very demanding. Most "traditional" artists only bother with learning one-point perspective and two-point perspective, but the more complicated and freeing three-point perspective is a mainstay of comic book art.

As you finish your perspective drawings, you should also take into account "atmospheric" perspective. This means that since there's more atmosphere between your eyes and the tree half a mile away from you compared to the distance there is between your eyes and the tree you're leaning against, the two trees are going to appear different. Closer objects have bolder colors, as well as more contrast between their lightest and darkest areas. Notice how the near cacti are a richer green color than the distant one. In pen and ink art, this usually means that closer objects are drawn with thicker, bolder lines, while the more distant objects are rendered with thinner, more uniform lines.

environment versus background

In fantasy art and comic books (whether it's superhero, science fiction, slice-of-life or anything else), the artist creates worlds. When depicting these worlds in your artwork, don't settle for having just backgrounds.

Environment is a word of weight and importance. *Background* is a word that describes something throwaway. When I changed how I referred to and thought of the buildings, cars, etc. in my drawings, they suddenly became more important to me. I was instantly more committed to creating the "environment" well and to getting it right, than I ever was to just drawing "backgrounds." And suddenly those tedious "backgrounds" weren't a chore to do anymore. They were fun and engaging to draw.

Drawing an environment rather than a background is more than having your character lean on a table instead of standing in front of it (although that certainly helps). There are great "talking head" shots where the background, even though we never see a point of contact between it and the characters, is definitely environment. These scenes give a sense of place, a sense of space and they subtly affect the characters. The scene wouldn't be the same in a different location. The *characters* wouldn't be the same in a different location.

Your characters need fully developed "environments" with which they can interact and environments that affect them.

Environments Affect Characters
This character is about to sit down in a booth at a diner. You can tell the place makes him uncomfortable by his facial expression and the way he positions himself in relation to the table, the cook and the waitress. This is a more subtle (and sublime) way to turn an ordinary setting into an environment.

Boring Background
Two people are sitting in a truck while an artificial landscape scrolls behind them to simulate movement. That's serious background. They don't care what it is; I don't care what it is. Two talking heads in front of some pretty scene, same thing: background.

Exciting Environment
On the other hand, look at kung fu movie geniuses like Jackie Chan bouncing off walls, moving tables and leaping off balconies. That's not background—it's too integral to the scene and to the characters. The characters interact with it; they are affected by it.

Horizon and Vanishing Point

The two most important terms to know in perspective drawing are *horizon* and *vanishing point*.

The horizon is an imaginary line representing the boundary between the ground and the sky. If you're standing on the beach, looking out at the ocean, that long line where the sea stops and the sky starts is the horizon. The horizon line is the most important building block in perspective drawing.

Vanishing points, usually located on the horizon line, are the other key building blocks for a successful perspective drawing. They are the imaginary points where parallel lines come together and meet far off in the distance. Imagine standing on a set of train tracks that stretch out as far as the eye can see. The two tracks would seem to get closer and closer together, finally merging at a vanishing point. The number of vanishing points required to make a drawing depends on the drawing itself. It could be one, or it could be 73 (or any other random number), but probably somewhere in between.

However, horizon and vanishing point aren't the only terms you need to know when learning about perspective. There's a good chunk of other terms worth noting.

Terms to Know

Parallel: Running in the same direction as. (For example, the line forming the top of a square is parallel to the line at the bottom.)

Perpendicular: Running in the opposite direction as or at a 90-degree angle to. (For example, the line forming the side of a square is perpendicular to the line at the bottom.)

90-Degree Angle/Right Angle: The most common angle in the man-made world. The sides of a square or rectangle meet at right angles.

45-Degree Angle: A 45-degree angle is half of a 90-degree angle. Draw a line diagonally across the corners of a square, and it will make a 45-degree angle with the sides of the square.

Plane: A straight, flat surface such as the top of a cube or a wall.

Ellipse: An oval shape used for drawing circles in perspective.

Horizontal: Depending on the context, lines that are either parallel to the ground or parallel to the bottom edge of the paper you're drawing on.

Vertical: Depending on the context, lines that are either straight up and down (perpendicular to the ground), or parallel to the side edges of the paper you're drawing on.

Image Area: The drawing itself, intended to be seen by the viewer. This doesn't include extra paper needed to draw vanishing points.

Picture Plane: Related to the image area, it's the imaginary plane of glass the viewer is looking through to see the scene you are drawing.

Viewer: The imaginary person or camera that is seeing the scene you are drawing.

Line of Sight: An imaginary line drawn from the viewer's eye in the direction he or she is looking.

Diagonal Vanishing Point (DVP): A special vanishing point placed to find lines at 45-degree angles to the main vanishing point(s). The DVP is very useful in making sure squares are actually square.

Magic Spot: A spot in a perspective drawing that can be used to find new vanishing points that are consistent with the established ones.

Recede: To go away from the viewer in space.

Orthogonal: Any line that converges at a vanishing point. This is also known as a receding line.

Receding Line: Another way of saying orthogonal—any line that converges at a vanishing point.

Bird's-Eye: A scene viewed from high above.

Worm's-Eye: A scene viewed from below.

Cone of Vision: A measurement of how much of a scene the drawing shows. Imagine the tip of a giant ice-cream cone pointing out of a camera's lens. The wider that cone of vision, the more of the scene you can see, but perspective drawings look distorted if the cone gets too wide and shows too much stuff.

five types of perspective

Perspective drawing for comics is half believable realism and half cinematography, that is, picking the right "camera angles" to reinforce the storytelling. We're all familiar with some different perspective techniques: a worm's-eye shot from below to show an imposing figure; a bird's-eye shot to show a character's reaction to overwhelming odds; or a long, wide shot to maintain a character's feelings of isolation.

All camera angles fall into different types of perspective drawing.

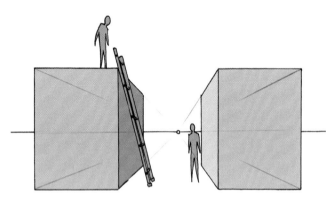

◐ *One-Point Perspective*
One-point is the easiest and simplest type of perspective. It's used to draw scenes we are viewing head-on, such as looking straight down a street or directly into a tunnel.

◑ *Two-Point Perspective*
Two-point perspective is much more free. It allows viewers to look all around the scene as long as they're looking at things more or less at the same level, rather than looking up or down at something.

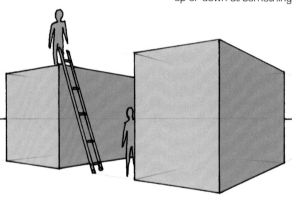

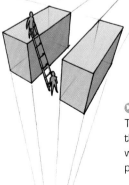

◕ *Three-Point Perspective*
Three-point perspective throws limits to the wind, enabling the viewer to look up, down, left, right or at any angle we want (except those that need to be drawn with one- or two-point perspective instead).

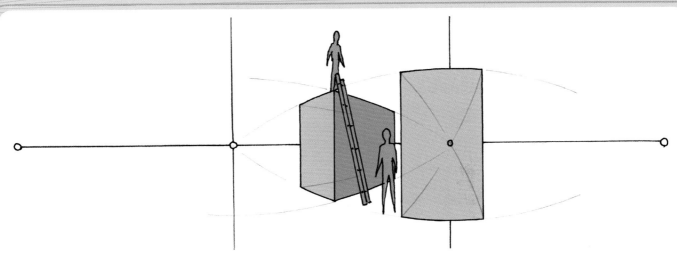

Curvilinear Perspective Terms

Vanishing Point Pair: In curvilinear perspective, vanishing points usually work in pairs. Curved lines arc out from one vanishing point and end up at another, creating a pair.

Arc: A curving line (technically one that's actually a part of the outside edge of a circle).

Connecting Line: A straight line drawn to connect a vanishing point pair. Arcs between vanishing point pairs bend away from this straight line.

Bisecting Line: A line that goes directly between two vanishing points, perpendicular to the line connecting those two points.

⟳ Curvilinear Perspective: Four-Point Perspective

Four-point perspective is the curvilinear equivalent of two-point perspective. Here we can look at objects on our own level from any angle we want, and take in a good wide view of them rather than having to back away from them to fit them in the picture like we do for two-point perspective. Since four-point perspective is the most difficult to grasp, we'll discuss it last.

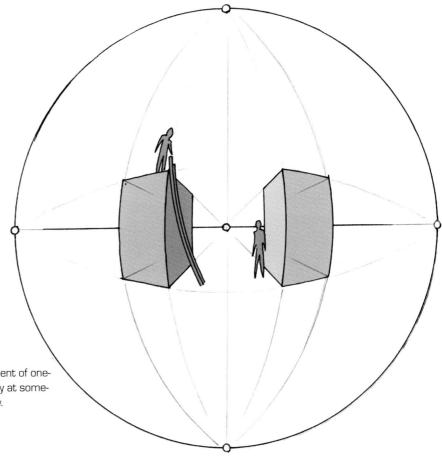

⟳ Curvilinear Perspective: Five-Point Perspective

Five-point perspective is the curvilinear equivalent of one-point perspective. Again, you're looking directly at something, but unlike one-point, you get a wide view.

CHAPTER TWO

ONE-POINT PERSPECTIVE

You're on the tracks, shrinking

from the oncoming train, or crawling into a ventilation system to chase bug-eyed monsters, and it's time to draw in one-point perspective. One-point is the simplest of all the perspectives, and is a great place to try out all the concepts and tricks you'll need for the fancier camera angles. But it's not just the easy way out, one-point images have an impact all their own. The first perspective drawings in the Renaissance were all in one-point perspective, and you can borrow their classical majesty for that perfect shot.

In one-point perspective, the viewer is looking flat-on at the objects in question. This means the nearest face of a rectangular box is parallel to the picture plane (and perpendicular to the line of sight).

All lines parallel to the line of sight will recede to a lone central vanishing point. The lines that make up that front face of the box (and all planes parallel to it) don't recede at all, so if it's a square, you draw a square, if it's a circle; you draw a circle, and so on.

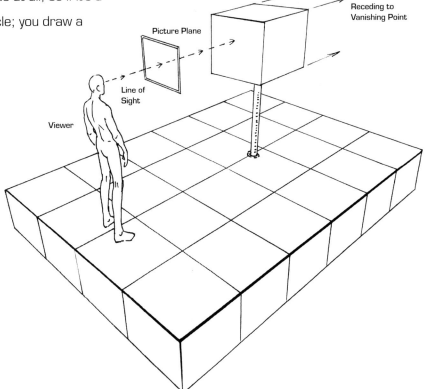

Receding to
Vanishing Point

Picture Plane

Line of
Sight

Viewer

draw a box in one-point perspective

1 Draw a horizon line and place the vanishing point (VP) in the middle. Use a T-square and/or triangle to make sure the line is perfectly horizontal.

Next, draw the front plane of the box. In one-point perspective, the box's plane is parallel to the picture plane, so nothing converges. Use your triangle/T-square to draw a simple rectangle. Make it nice and bold.

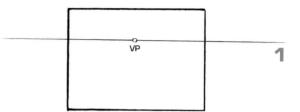

1

2 Pull a line from each corner of the rectangle back to the vanishing point. Use one of the basic principles of drawing on white paper: Darker, thicker lines seem to come forward in space. Draw nice and dark as you start from the corners, but ease up the pressure as you pull back to the vanishing point.

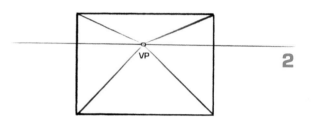

2

3 Draw a horizontal line that connects two of the receding lines (also called the orthogonals). This line should be kind of dark, but notably lighter than the lines that make up the front plane of the box.

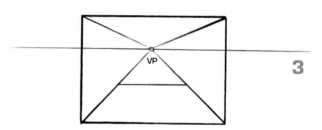

3

4 Finish by drawing vertical lines from the intersection of the horizontal line and the receding lines. Where they connect with the other receding lines, draw a second horizontal line and you've completed a form in one-point perspective.

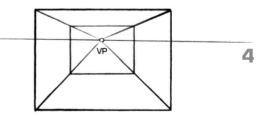

4

5 Erase any construction lines you don't want. Do any rendering or inking you think the form needs to help it "exist in space."

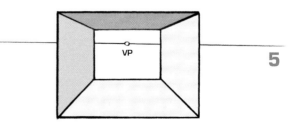

5

Using a Triangle or T-square

Triangles and T-squares make it easy to draw the vertical and horizontal lines you need for drawing in not just one-point perspective, but two-, three-, four-, and five-point as well. But lining up the triangle with the edge of the paper every time you want or need a vertical or horizontal will waste your time. There are two basic options.

1. You can tape your paper to the drawing surface, using the T-square to line it up with the edge of the surface. Then use the T-square to draw horizontal lines, and use the triangle resting on the T-square to draw verticals.

2. Have a nice, straight, raised lip or edge on the drawing surface. Put your paper against that edge, and your triangle on the edge to draw the verticals, and just rotate the paper to its other side to draw the horizontals. This is the easier option.

Now draw several boxes grouped together following the same rules of one-point perspective used to draw a single box.

1 Draw the front planes of the boxes. Put rectangles anywhere you want them.

2 Pull receding lines to the vanishing point and draw the back planes of the boxes just as you did for the single box exercise.

3 Finish up your forms and get rid of the construction lines. Whether you're finishing up your boxes in pencil or ink, make the lines closest to the viewer thicker and bolder, and let the lines get thinner and lighter as they recede to help your forms "exist in space."

Cleaning up Construction Lines

Erasing out all the little lines you don't want from between all the ones you do want is pretty difficult, but you have a lot of options.

You can draw the construction lines so lightly a kneaded erase will pick them up but leave the darker lines of the form. Or you can draw construction lines in a different color from the final forms.

There are two other methods quite popular in comic art:

1. Do the construction on one piece of paper, then overlay the final art (using tracing paper or vellum or heavier paper and a lightbox) to draw the final forms.

2. Do the construction in pencil, then ink the final forms, and finally erase all the pencil lines (like in this example).

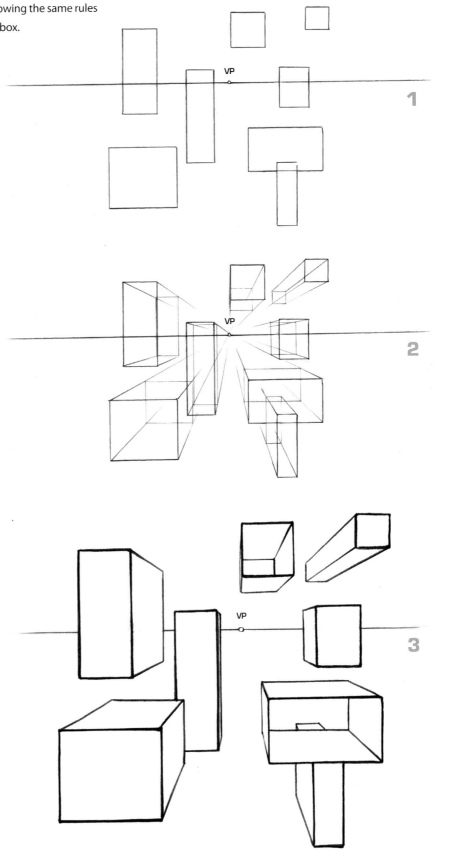

divide space

X-Marks-the-Spot

When you're drawing complicated objects, the ability to divide the shape up evenly is vital. If you want to draw multistory buildings and keep the stories the same height, or find the middle of a rectangle so that you can draw a set of double doors, "X-marks-the-spot" is the best trick to have in your toolbox.

1

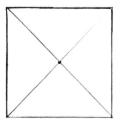

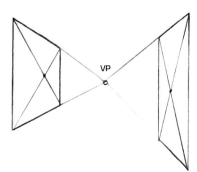

Receding in Perspective

VP

2

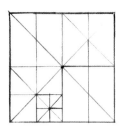

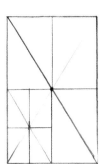

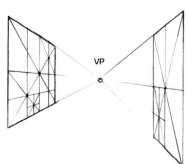

Receding in Perspective

VP

1 Straight lines connecting opposite corners of any rectangle or square will always cross in the center—even when the rectangle is receding in perspective. These lines are called diagonals.

2 Divide each rectangle into four smaller rectangles. For the rectangles parallel to the picture plane, draw horizontal and vertical lines through the center. For the receding rectangles, you'll need to use lines receding to the vanishing point as well as true verticals (or horizontals depending on what way the rectangle is facing). Repeat as needed to divide any of the new rectangles. How far do you want the rectangle divided? It's up to you and the object you're drawing. A pair of double doors only need one X to find the center vertical, but windows made up of many panes of glass will need more.

3

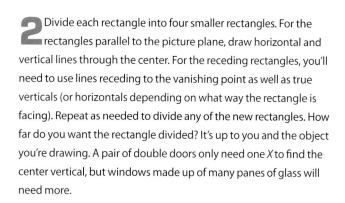

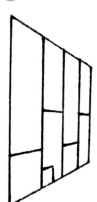

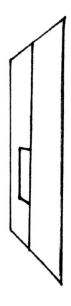

3 Get rid of any lines, horizontal, vertical or diagonal, you don't need and leave all the divisions you do.

Once you've divided up one side of an object—say the front of an office building—it's handy to be able to move the measurements around to the other sides of the object, rather than having to re-divide each face of the object.

1 Since the front plane of the box is parallel to the picture plane, you can use a ruler to make any measurements you want. Make equal divisions on the front face for a grid. Pick up those divisions at the edges and take each one back to the vanishing point and you have perfectly consistent divisions in perspective.

2 Now draw a diagonal line as you did in X-marks-the-spot. Either diagonal will work, but drawing the one that will intersect the receding lines closer to a 90-degree angle will make it easier to keep the divisions accurate.

3 Draw vertical lines through the intersections of the receding lines and the diagonals. The neat thing is that this works for transferring any divisions or measurements, not just equal ones. Any proportions measured out on the front face will be duplicated in perfect perspective when they're transferred by the diagonal line.

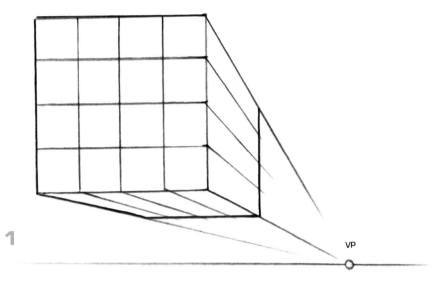

1

VP

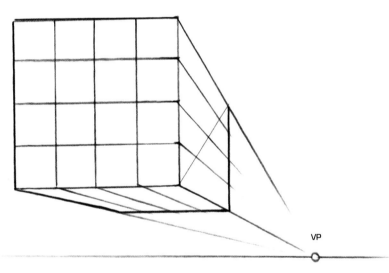

2

VP

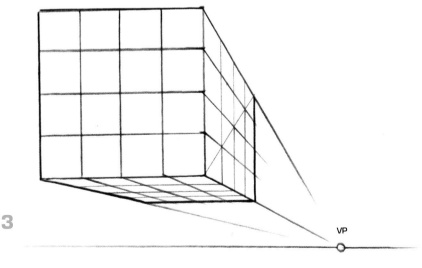

3

VP

the diagonal vanishing point

Nine times out of ten, all you need for one-point perspective are the principles just discussed. You can eyeball the proportions and wing things, and it looks great. Unless you're an architect, you don't need accuracy, just believability. But every once in awhile you will draw something that's tough to wing. Your eye tells you it's wrong, but it won't tell you what you have to do to make it right. That's when you need a few more tricks in your toolbox.

The diagonal vanishing point lets you draw perfect squares in perspective. It makes it easy to measure things as they go back in space to ensure that you don't draw a car that's 8 feet (3m) wide but 50 feet (15m) long. It lets you draw accurate and believable tile floors or regular fence posts.

The diagonal vanishing point also tells you how far the viewer is from the objects in the picture. Distant diagonal vanishing points (DVPs) put the viewer far away, flatten the scene and reduce perspective distortions. Closer in, the DVPs bring the viewer closer to the action, but increase perspective distortions.

In one-point perspective there are two diagonal vanishing points, each one on the horizon line and spaced equally apart from the vanishing point. This exercise on creating a tile floor will give you lots of practice with diagonal vanishing points.

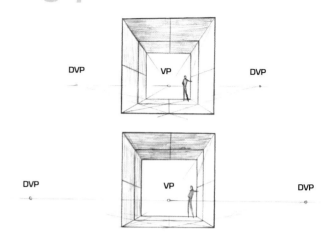

⌒ *Closing in on the Action*

These boxes are the same size and proportions; it's only the viewer that's different. The top box has the viewer quite close, showing us more of the interior walls. The bottom box has the point of view much farther out—the drawing equivalent of using a long lens in photography. The first example would be the equivalent of using a shorter lens, maybe even a wide-angle.

1 Draw a horizon line and place the vanishing point (VP) in the middle. Measure out the diagonal vanishing points (DVPs) to make sure they're the same distance from the VP. Draw the front edge of a tile near the center of the picture, and take the corners of that tile back to the VP. You've established the width of the tile, and now you need to make it the same depth. Draw a line from the front corner of the tile to the opposite DVP. You can use either DVP. Here I've used both.

2 Draw a horizontal line at the point where the lines receding to the VP and the line receding to the DVP intersect. Congrats! You've just drawn a perfect square in perspective.

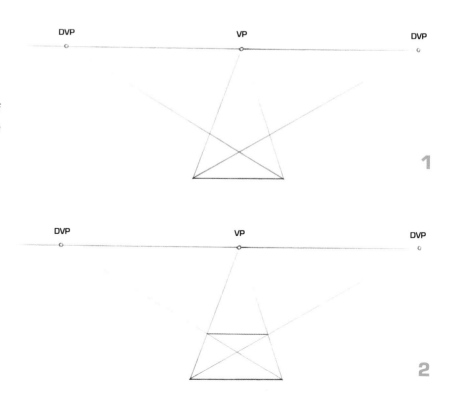

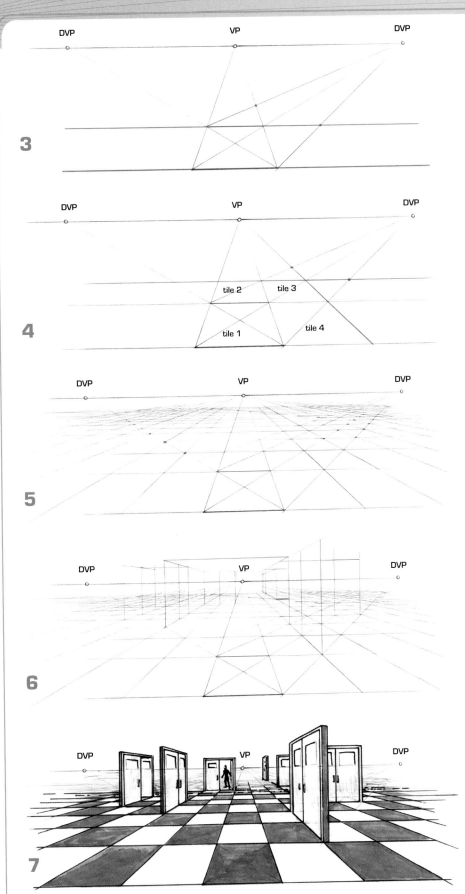

3 Extend the horizontal lines of your tile on both sides. Then take lines back to either DVP from the tile corners. Mark where the lines to the DVP cross the line to the vanishing point.

4 Wherever the receding lines to the DVP cross the horizontal lines, you'll draw a new receding line to the VP. Wherever the lines receding to the DVP cross the lines receding to the VP, you'll draw a new horizontal. Place two new lines in and you now have four tiles instead of just one.

5 Repeat this process until you've filled up the necessary space. Pull new lines to the DVP from the tile corners, pull new horizontals and lines to the VP from the intersections of the DVP and VP lines. It's a bit of juggling back and forth to get it done (VP, DVP, horizontal), but as you get into it, you'll see where you can lay in just one new line to the DVP to create dozens of new horizontals and receding lines.

6 In addition to a nice tile floor, you now have regular divisions throughout the entire space, making it easy to draw consistently sized objects no matter how close or far away they are. Take lines up from the grid to draw the frames for double doors. Keep the height of each door consistent by pulling new receding lines to the vanishing point and using new horizontals to transfer the height of one door to any place in space. The closer you get to the horizon, the harder it is to be accurate in the divisions. Measure as much as you can at a far distance from the horizon.

7 Take that solid foundation and render your scene.

Draw a Scene in One-Point Perspective

1 On a large piece of paper, place your horizon, vanishing point and diagonal vanishing points. To create the railroad tracks, draw two receding lines back to the vanishing point. Use the DVP to start dividing the track up regularly as described on pages 22-23.

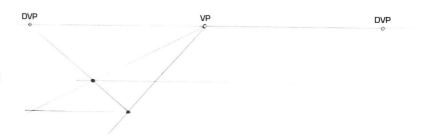

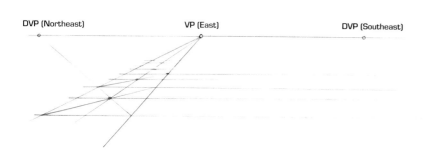

2 Pull to the opposite DVP point to get an X-marks-the-spot to draw a construction line parallel to and exactly between the two tracks. This will let you divide up twice as many horizontal lines. Since the horizontal lines are going to be the ties of the train track, they need to be closer together than the spread of the rails to look accurate. Remember, VPs and DVPs don't represent places, but directions. So if the VP is east, the DVPs will be northeast and southeast.

3 The horizontals from the first track will mark the rails for the second track. Use the DVP to pull a line across those horizontals to make sure this track is the same width as the first.

Draw vertical lines up from the tracks to start the train. Proportions are important in order for it to look like a real train. This is a good place for a reference photo or a model train to help you out. Even if you don't copy the train exactly, the bits you use will add to the believability. Trains are wider than the tracks, so much of the train will extend past the verticals you've drawn. Draw a square up from the tracks and find its center to place a couple of circles for the front of the train.

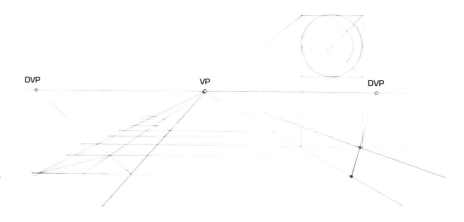

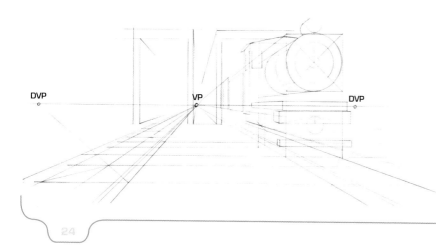

4 Start building the shape of your train. Pull lines back to the VP from the circle to build the cylinder of the train. Use another, smaller circle to cap off the end of the cylinder. Build boxes to block out the shape of the train. Use X-marks-the-spot to keep the masses of the train centered over the tracks. Lay in the basic shape of the twin trestle bridges behind the train.

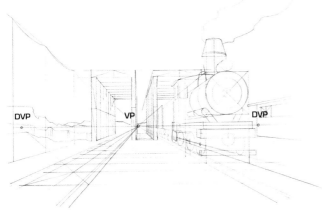

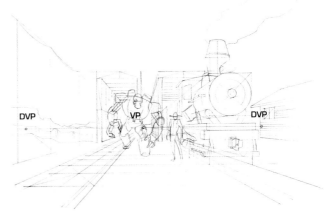

5 Lay in the basic block of the train's smokestack. Use X-marks-the-spot to divide the trestle bridges into their individual trusses. Place the basic shape of the building and its window off to the right. Place telegraph poles to the left. Sketch in circles for the train's wheels. Sketch in the irregular shapes of the background terrain, remembering that in a flat plane like this things will approach towards the horizon, but the uneven actual horizon won't drop below the ideal horizon line at any point.

6 Add any further details you want to the telegraph poles, the house and the train.

Place the general shape of the figures. Use the train to set the height of the figures, remembering that a horizontal line from their feet over to the train will show how far forward they are relative to the train and another horizontal line from the top of the head will show how tall they are relative to the train.

The drawing is pretty busy by now, so it might be easier to work the figures out on a tracing paper overlay.

7 Render your finishing details to the scene. You don't need to use the vanishing point and a ruler to add each detail to the train, just keep an eye on the grid of perspective lines you've drawn around the details you've added to help the little pieces agree with the perspective of the bigger forms. If you're inking, erase all pencil lines to get rid of the unwanted construction lines.

In a Dry, Dusty Town

Homework

To really grasp the lessons of one-point perspective, find a room that has good rectangular shapes in it (beds, dressers, coffee tables, etc.). Sit centered to the wall, and face the room flat-on. Draw what you see!

CHAPTER THREE

TWO-POINT PERSPECTIVE

With the lessons of one-point

perspective safely under your belt, it's time to move on to two-point perspective. The vast majority of the scenes you draw will probably be in two-point. One-point has classical simplicity, three-point has extra impact, but two-point is the workhorse of straight-line perspectives.

In basic two-point perspective the viewer is looking at an object that is rotated so that one corner is closer than all others. But the viewer is not looking up or down at the object. The picture plane is still at eye level. Vertical lines stay vertical, but all lines parallel to the ground now recede to two separate vanishing points on the horizon.

At any given time, walking through our daily lives, the scenes we're seeing are usually in two-point perspective. We tend to spend our time looking straight across, rather than up or down (which would put us in three-point), but most often we're not looking exactly square on to our surroundings (which would put us in one-point).

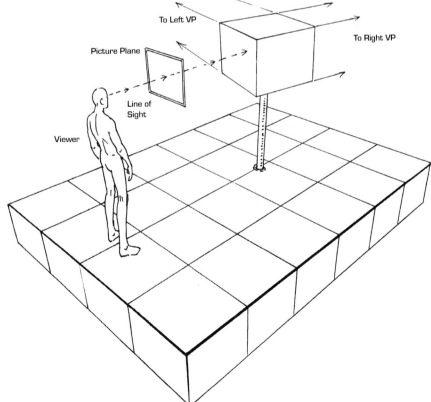

To Left VP

To Right VP

Picture Plane

Line of
Sight

Viewer

draw a box in two-point perspective

1 Set your horizon line with a vanishing point at each end. Draw a bold, vertical line for the closest corner of the box.

2 Pull receding lines to each vanishing point back from the top and bottom of the vertical line.

3 To create the edges of the box, draw vertical lines connecting the receding lines. These vertical lines are your left- and right-side corners.

4 Draw the back sides of the box by pulling receding lines from the top and bottom of the side corners to the opposite vanishing points.

5 Finish the box with the back edge, a vertical line drawn through the intersections of the receding lines.

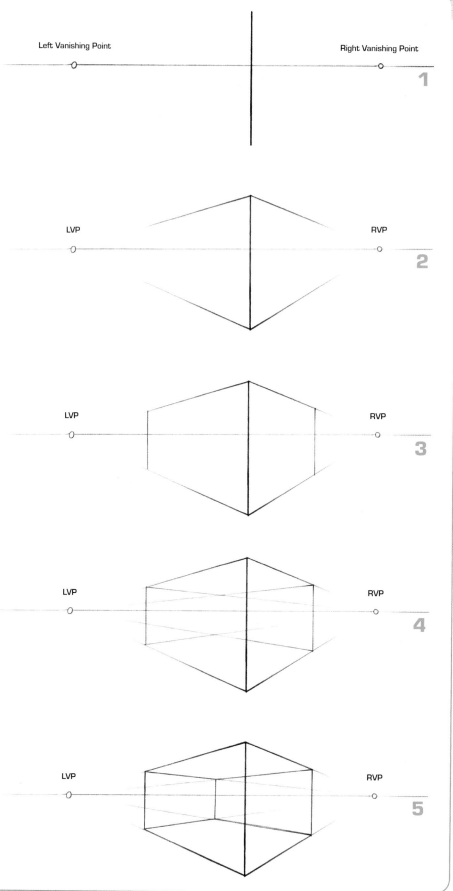

1 With your horizon and vanishing points in place, draw multiple vertical lines.

2 Follow the same steps as with the single box to draw an array of boxes in two-point perspective. Clean up any unwanted construction lines.

It's important to remember that vanishing points represent directions, not places. So if your left vanishing point is east, your right vanishing point would be south.

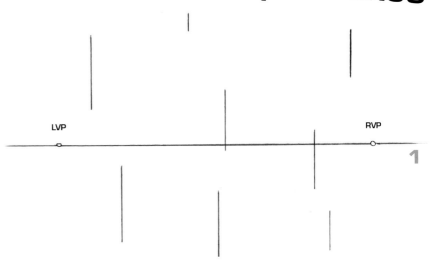

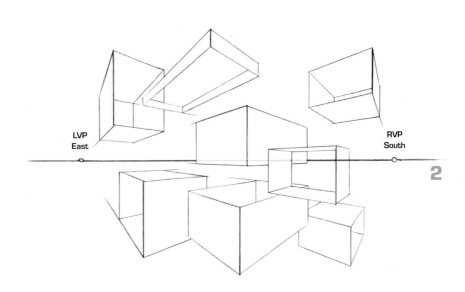

⊘ Dividing Space in Two-Point Perspective

Dividing space in two-point perspective works just the same as in one-point. Use X-marks-the-spot (page 20) to find the center and pull receding lines or draw verticals through that center as appropriate.

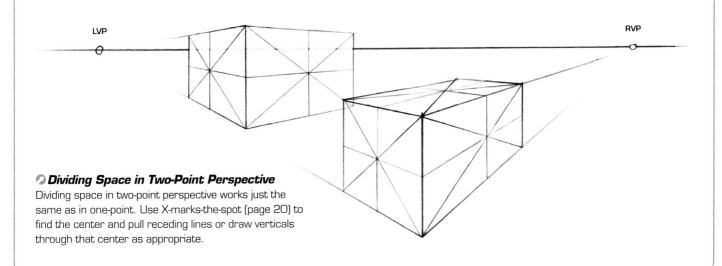

the diagonal vanishing point

Once again, the basic concepts of drawing a box, multiple boxes and dividing space will give you most of what you need to draw scenes in two-point perspective. But sometimes you need that extra accuracy and consistency to build up your believability—you just can't wing it.

So the diagonal vanishing point (DVP) returns for the rescue. With the increased flexibility of two-point perspective, placing the DVP becomes a little trickier, but there's an easy way to do it and once the DVP is in place, it's just as easy to use as the DVP in one-point perspective. First, get a big piece of paper, a triangle and a straightedge.

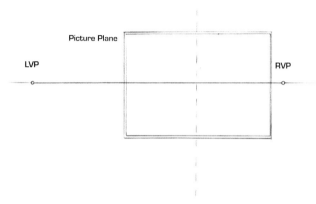

1 Draw your horizon line and place your VPs on it. Approximate where the boundaries of your image will be. (One or both VPs likely won't be within the boundaries of your final drawing.) Here the left VP is farther away from the image edge, so the receding left planes will be seen more head-on, and the receding right planes will be seen at a more extreme angle. Sketch a vertical line through the center of the picture plane, dropping it below the image area.

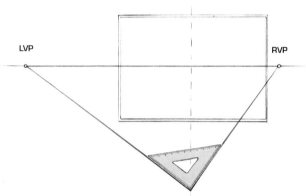

2 Using the straightedge and triangle, find the one point on the vertical center line where lines from the two VPs meet at a 90-degree angle. If you have a large triangle, place a straightedge against one side to extend its reach and float the corner of the triangle slowly up and down the vertical center line, gradually rotating in until you've found the spot where the two legs of the triangle point at both VPs at the same time. Mark that point and the receding lines that lead to it.

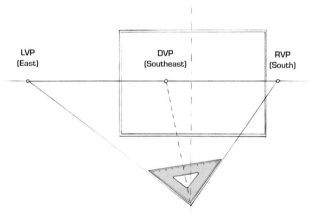

3 Draw a line from the 90-degree angle up to the horizon, exactly between the two receding lines at 45 degrees. To do this, use a 45-degree drafting triangle rotated to put the point in the corner. The diagonal vanishing point is where that 45-degree line meets the horizon. Remember, the vanishing points represent directions, not locations.

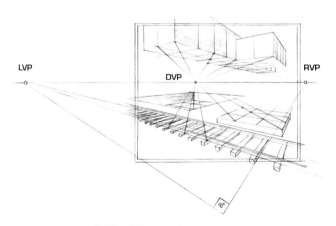

↻ The Diagonal Vanishing Point in Action
Once you've placed the DVP, its use is identical to the use of the DVP in one-point perspective (see pages 22-23). Pull a line from any intersection back to the DVP, and you can draw a perfect square, or a whole grid of them.

Diagonal vanishing points are great, but they aren't the only game in town. Sometimes you need a consistent shape that isn't a square. That's where special vanishing points (SVPs) come into play. Remember, anything that can be lined up will draw lines that converge at a vanishing point.

LVP   RVP

Special Vanishing Point

1

Special Vanishing Point on the Horizon

1 We need to draw a series of consistently sized rectangular tiles. Using your horizon and two vanishing points, draw one tile that looks the right size near the center of your image.

Extend a diagonal through the corners of the rectangle to the horizon. Where that line meets the horizon is the "special vanishing point." The tiles are parallel to the ground, so all lines across the tiles, to diagonal VPs or to special VPs, will converge on the horizon.

2 Using the special vanishing point just as you would a diagonal vanishing point, draw a series of consistently sized tiles.

3 Draw the rest of your scene. Your two vanishing points and special vanishing point have allowed you to map out the space you need for a convincing drawing.

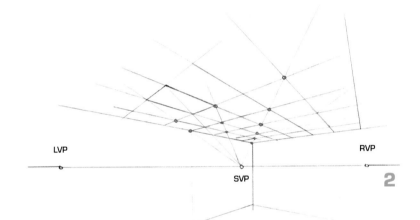

LVP   RVP

SVP

2

3

31

Special Vanishing Point off the Horizon

We can use special vanishing points to divide vertical space as well. Since these rectangles are on a vertical plane converging to a single vanishing point, the special vanishing points for their diagonals will be directly above or below that vanishing point. You can use multiple special vanishing points for different sizes. Here, the wider windows are marked out by taking a receding line to the lower special vanishing point 1 (SVP1). The narrower spaces between the windows use special vanishing point 2 (SVP2). Remember the special vanishing point is great for marking out any regularly spaced divisions (e.g., picket fences, telephone poles). Don't think of them as being just for rectangles.

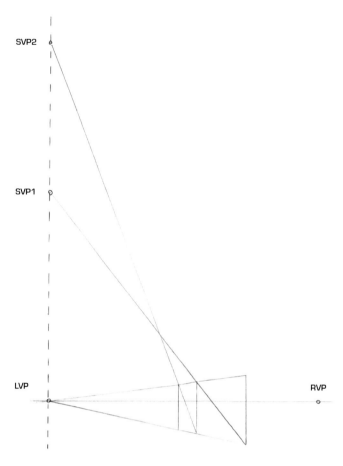

1 Draw two rectangles following the instructions on page 28, and take their diagonals back until they cross a vertical line that runs through the vanishing point used to draw the rectangles. Where these lines cross are your special vanishing points.

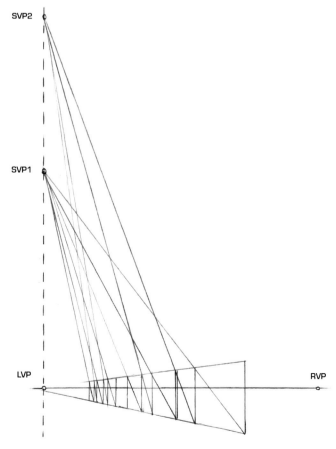

2 Alternate between special vanishing point 1 and special vanishing point 2 to draw the series of windows across the face of the building.

In perspective drawings, the vanishing points are often a large distance from the edge of the actual image. They need to be, or the image is badly distorted. One handy trick is to tape your drawing paper down to a large sheet of cheap posterboard. This allows you to draw all the vanishing points and special vanishing points at any distance you need. The posterboard can be used over and over until you've drawn too many horizons and vanishing points on the board and it becomes confusing to use. Then just turn the sheet over and start again on the other side or get a new sheet of posterboard.

3 Render and clean up. Don't use the ruler too much in the final drawing, especially when drawing older brick buildings—you get more character and texture when you freehand the finished lines.

Two-Point Perspective

LVP
RVP
DVP
VP
DVP
DVP

One-Point Perspective

Using What You Already Know

You actually already know how to draw one special case of the DVP in two-point perspective: the 45-degree scene, where the line of sight intersects the main object at 45 degrees (one-point perspective would be a 90-degree scene). Take the central VP and two DVPs for one-point perspective and switch roles, making the DVPs the new left and right VPs and the old central VP the new DVP. Voila!

Draw a Scene in Two-Point Perspective

Now it's time to put two-point perspective to work. We need a moody street-corner good-bye in a film noir city. Two-point perspective is tailor-made for eye-level street corner shots. You'll need your two VPs and the DVP to map out the regular divisions in the pavement and keep the width of doors and windows consistent as they go back in space.

1 Plan out everything by sketching your scene. Without a plan in place, laying out the vanishing points and drawing your receding lines with a ruler is a sure path to frustration. Don't worry about details. Focus on the general placement and content of the image.

2 Using your sketch as a guide, decide on a placement for the horizon and your vanishing points (which really represent directions: north and east in this case). Lay them in, find your diagonal vanishing points (see page 30) and work out the grid for the sidewalk. A grid will give nice, regular divisions to the sidewalk—and it's really handy for drawing consistently sized doors and windows.

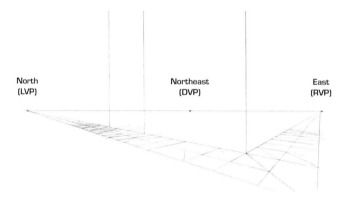

3 Use your vanishing points to block in the major forms of the buildings, the elevated train and its tracks. Use the sidewalk grid to help keep doors and windows consistently sized. If you have an extra piece to draw, such as the sign that juts out from the corner of the building, just treat the diagonal vanishing point like a VP. It's so small you can safely fake the second vanishing point.

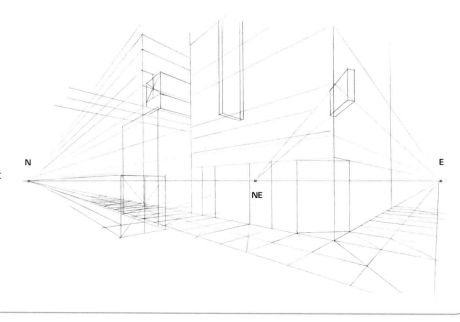

N

E

4 Add detail to the basic forms. Use the tried-and-true X-marks-the-spot method (page 20) wherever you need to find the center of an object (e.g., sliding windows or the front of the train).

Lay in your figures, remembering that the horizon line will intersect people of the same height at the same point no matter where they're standing.

5 Render and clean up. Sometimes an illustration is made by what's left out rather than what's put in. Don't succumb to the temptation to keep every division in the pavement, or every edge of a window. The eye doesn't see that way. Keep the structure accurate, but let the forms break and disappear—the eye will enjoy filling in those spaces.

Midnight in the Roaring Twenties

perspective doesn't care which way is up

Up until now, the horizon line of the drawing has been analogous to the actual horizon of the globe. But it doesn't have to be! If we rotate that horizon line to a vertical, it opens up a whole new set of possibilities.

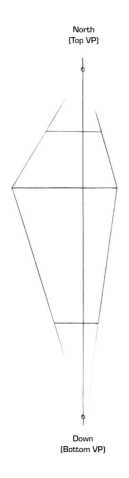

North
(Top VP)

Down
(Bottom VP)

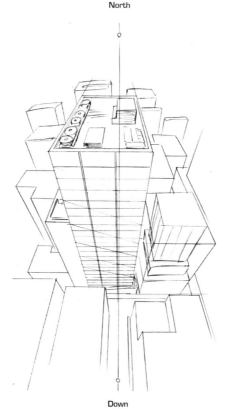

North

Down

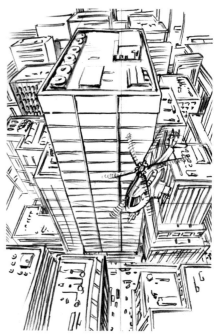

1 Lay out your vertical "horizon" line and two vanishing points. The vanishing points are still 90 degrees apart from each other, but instead of being, say north and east, they represent north and down (or even north and up if you want). The vanishing points can represent any two directions that are 90 degrees apart from each other. Draw a box for your primary form (see page 28).

2 In general, skyscrapers are just stacks of rectangles. Lay out your cityscape. Planes that recede to the top vanishing point (north) represent horizontal surfaces, like streets or rooftops. Planes that recede to the bottom vanishing point (down) represent vertical surfaces. Instead of vertical lines that don't converge, we now have horizontal lines that don't converge.

3 Render your scene. Don't let all the buildings have the same finish to them, and use things like banks of air conditioners, water tanks and utility structures to break up the rooftops and make the buildings more interesting and believable. This rotated horizon trick is a great way to give that vertigo-inducing sense of height and altitude. It's a looooong way down to that street.

When Winging It Goes Wrong!

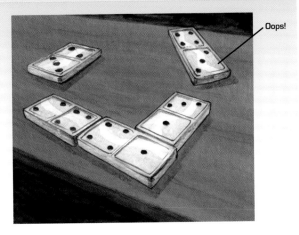

Oops!

These lessons work great as long as everything faces the same way, but we know that's not always the case. See how the domino in the upper right-hand corner is out of proportion to the other dominos? Placing one new VP by eye is easy, getting that second one in the right place is trickier. Objects drawn by a mismatched pair of vanishing points won't exist properly in the same space as the rest of the scene. One way to fix this problem is by rotating the scene's grid.

Two vanishing points will draw an infinite number of objects, but only objects that are facing the same direction. To populate a drawing with objects rotated at angles to each other, we need more vanishing points. But, sometimes you don't need to establish new vanishing points. Use your existing VPs and DVP to draw a standard grid in two-point perspective, and from that you can rotate new grids in space, creating a new set of accurate lines in a new perspective absolutely consistent with the first.

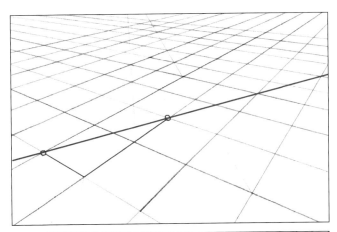

1 Pick a starting point on the corner of a tile and mark it. Trace one tile over and two tiles up on the grid and mark a second point. Draw a line that passes through both those points.

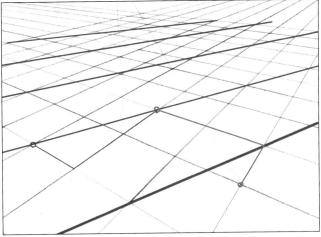

2 Draw a series of lines parallel to the line established in Step 1 by repeating Step 1 with new starting points.
   Now set up the perpendiculars of the grid. Pick a tile corner as a starting point (the ending point from Step 1 is a good point to use). Trace two tiles over and one tile back and mark the ending point.

3 Draw a line that passes through the points you marked in Step 2 to make a line perpendicular to the lines you drew in Steps 1 and 2. Repeat this process to complete the new grid, rotated from the first and drawn at the same distance from the viewer.

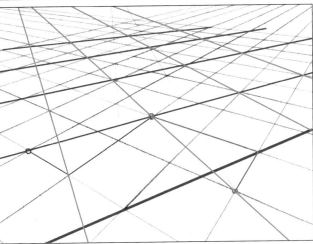

Drawing New Vanishing Points

The secret to drawing a pair of new vanishing points that agree with the original pair of vanishing points is the spot we used to find the diagonal vanishing point—the magic spot. The image's magic spot is where the lines from the vanishing points meet at a 90-degree angle (see page 30). At this one point, all angles are unchanged by perspective. Any angles measured from this point will be accurate and consistent with the rest of the image. With this trick of finding new vanishing points, we're not limited to objects that line up with the main VPs. We can draw anything from a spread of playing cards on a table to cars scattered on a highway. Let's put the theory into practice.

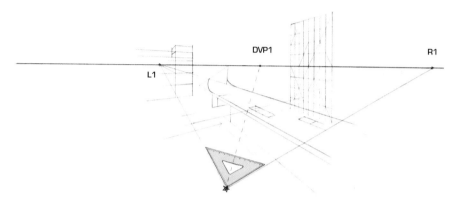

1 Start the scene. Locate the primary pair of vanishing points (L1 and R1) and construct the diagonal vanishing points for them (see page 30). Make special note of the intersection point (starred). This is the magic spot. Lay in the basic forms of the streets and buildings. (Note how the raised street converges at the horizon even after it turns.)

Draw the bases of the cars facing toward the primary vanishing points, using the diagonal vanishing point to divide the rectangles into measurable squares (in this case one square wide and a little less than three squares long).

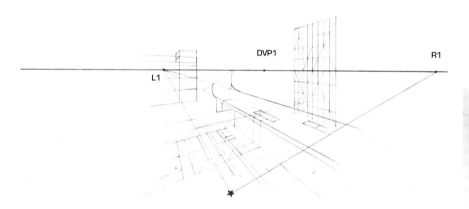

2 Extend one of the squares from the first car you drew to the edge of the road. Then draw vertical lines to bring the square's edges down to ground level and extend the lines farther (using receding lines to your first vanishing point on the right). Pull a line to the diagonal vanishing point across the lines and you've got a consistently sized square on a new plane. Work from this new square to measure out more car bases that are one square wide and almost three squares long.

Drawing Multiple Cars

Drawing cars is a challenge; they're complex shapes, and we're so familiar with them that our eyes easily notice when they're drawn wrong. When tackling a scene with multiple cars, differently rotated and consistent vanishing points are key. The diagonal vanishing points help even more.

Proportioning a car properly is important. You can use one car as a standard (especially if it's a cab or police car that will show up multiple times in a scene). The standard police cruiser is 2.75 times longer than it is wide, so using the DVP, we can draw rectangles that are 2¾ squares long, and 1 square wide.

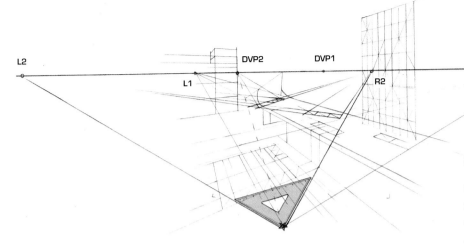

3 Draw a new set of vanishing points. Place your triangle on the magic spot and rotate it to whatever angle you want the new cars to be rotated to. Extend lines from the triangle; where they meet the horizon are your two new vanishing points (L2 and R2).

As usual, draw a line 45 degrees between your new vanishing points to place the new diagonal vanishing point (DVP2). Using this new set of vanishing points, draw new car bases, still one square wide and almost three squares long. Repeat the process of creating new cars as often as you want.

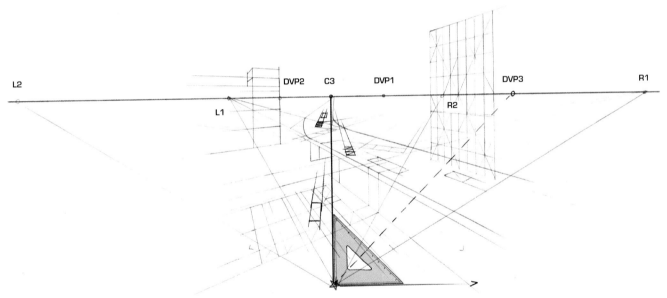

4 There is a special case when you place a vanishing point (C3) directly above the magic spot. This happens when the triangle points directly sideways to find the second vanishing point, which will never converge with the horizon.

At this point, you need to draw in one-point perspective because the viewer sees this section of the drawing flat-on. Measure a 45-degree angle from the vertical line at the magic spot that creates C3. Draw a line along this 45-degree angle, and where it crosses the horizon is the diagonal vanishing point (DVP3). Use C3 and DVP3 to draw more car bases in one-point perspective.

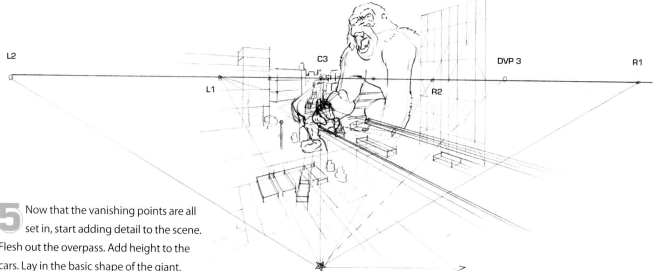

5 Now that the vanishing points are all set in, start adding detail to the scene. Flesh out the overpass. Add height to the cars. Lay in the basic shape of the giant, rampaging ape. Even though he's not a rectangle, he still obeys the laws of perspective—above the horizon line you're looking up at him, so you see a little more of the underside of his forms. Below the horizon you're looking down at him, so you see a little more of the topside of his forms. (This concept is covered fully on page 65.)

6 Tighten the scene. Only the police cruisers need to adhere to the measured rectangles—the other makes and models can float inside those rectangles, a little shorter or narrower, whatever's needed. (For tips on drawing cars see pages 68-69.) Remember the importance of leaving things out? Some of the cars you framed in would have cluttered the space behind the monkey's fist, so just leave them out.

Enlarging Your Constructions

On a drawing such as this example, the vanishing points are very far-flung. Even if you were working on a very large piece of paper, the actual image area is probably too small to work in comfortably. Once your construction is done, you can use a photocopier to increase the image area. (Forget the vanishing points, they've done their jobs.) Trace this enlargement (using tracing paper, vellum, or lightboxed bristol) and transfer it before rendering in color or ink.

Power Monkey

7 Render and clean up. If you're working in color, take atmospheric perspective into consideration. The farther away objects are, the lower their contrast will be (blacks will be more gray, and whites will be more gray), and they will pick up more tinges of sky color. The *In a Dry, Dusty Town* illustration on page 25 is another good example of atmospheric perspective.

Homework

Draw your room! Go to the same room you drew in the homework assignment for chapter two (on page 25), only this time set up so that you're not looking at a wall straight-on. Sit so you're facing at or toward a corner. Draw what you see!

CHAPTER FOUR

THREE-POINT PERSPECTIVE

And now you've arrived at the

ultimate in straight-line perspectives—three-point perspective. In one-point you can only look straight ahead, dead-on. In two-point you can look around, but not up or down. In three-point, you can look anywhere, which is a good thing. Obviously you need three-point for flying, swinging and leaping superheroes traipsing about the rooftops. But even for those little dialogue scenes, the freedom to throw in upshots and downshots, bird's-eye and worm's-eye, lets you bring in the variety you need to keep the scene interesting.

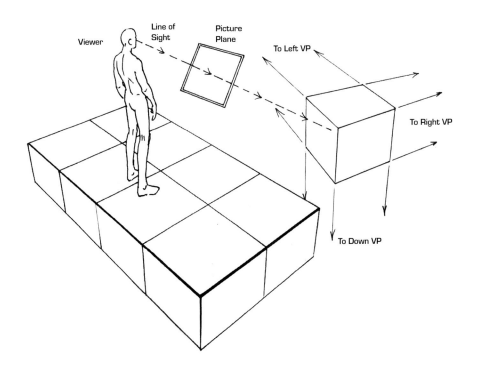

the unlimited box

1 Place the horizon line and two vanishing points as you do in two-point perspective. Now figure out where the third vanishing point goes. If you're looking down on the object, the third VP goes below the horizon; if you're looking up, it goes above it.

Place the third VP and draw two more horizon lines to connect all the VPs. Remember, the three VPs are all 90 degrees away from each other. If the one on the right is north, then the left one is west, and the bottom one is down. Left and right are pretty relative to our brains, but up and down are more important, and distortion in your verticals looks unsettling pretty quickly.

2 Draw the leading edges of the box. Pick a point to be the nearest point of the box. Draw lines radiating from this point back to each of the VPs.

3 Draw the silhouette of the box by pulling six more lines to the VPs to describe the edges of the box (two to the left, two to the right and two to the bottom).

4 Draw the hidden back of the box by pulling three more lines from the intersections of the outer edges. If you've kept everything pretty accurate, the three lines (one to each VP) should come together in one tight little point that is the farthest point of the box from the camera.

5 Use your perspective box skeleton to render your object.

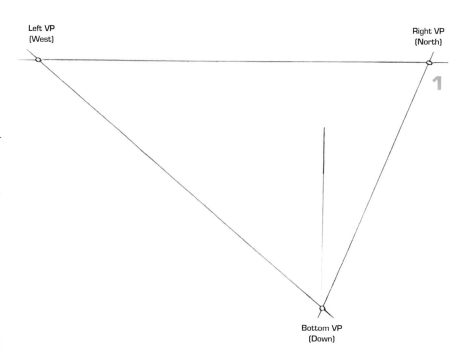

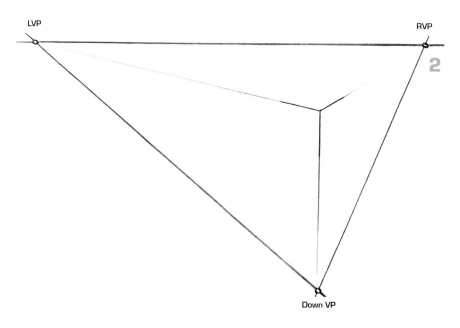

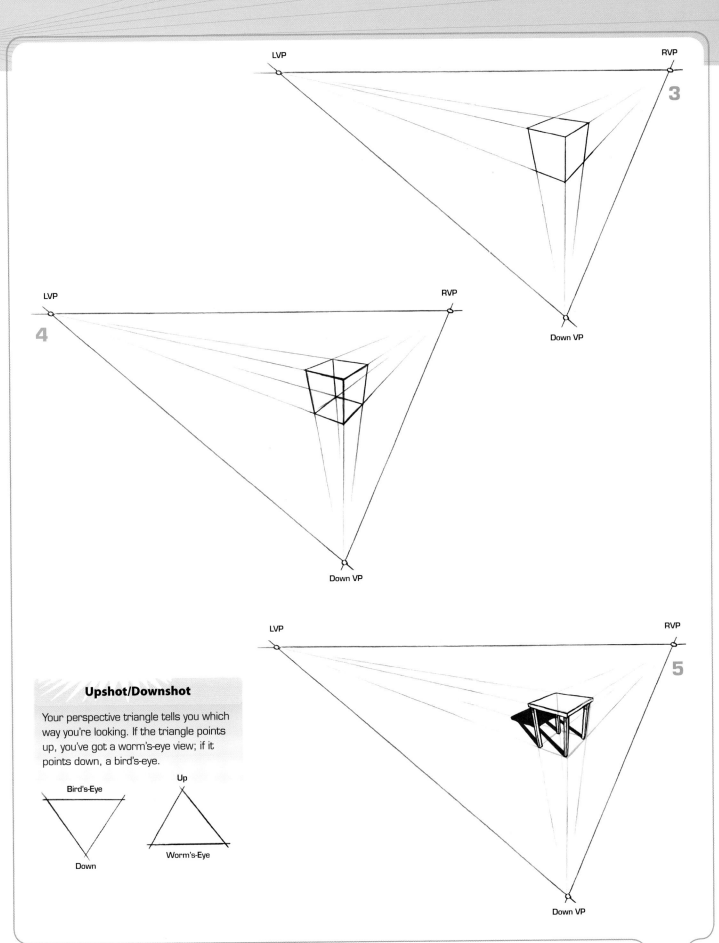

LVP

RVP

3

Down VP

LVP

RVP

4

Down VP

LVP

RVP

5

Upshot/Downshot

Your perspective triangle tells you which way you're looking. If the triangle points up, you've got a worm's-eye view; if it points down, a bird's-eye.

Bird's-Eye

Up

Down

Worm's-Eye

Down VP

diagonal vanishing points

The Unlimited Box exercise has taught you the basics of three-point perspective. The X-marks-the-spot trick from one-point and two-point (see page 20) works exactly the same in three-point. You can wing the rest.

However, if you need a little more accuracy to achieve believability in an image, three-point perspective has three diagonal vanishing points that can help.

Placing the diagonal vanishing points in three-point isn't any harder than placing them in two-point, but it is easier to get confused with all the competing sets of lines. So keep your head clear and sketch things in lightly so you can darken up what you need and erase or ignore the rest.

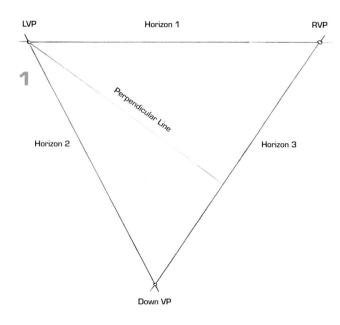

1 Create your horizon triangle. Draw a line perpendicular (90 degrees) to one of the horizons and have this line pass through the vanishing point opposite the horizon.

2 Repeat this process for the other two horizons and vanishing points. The perpendicular lines should cross at one point. This point is the center of vision. The closer the center of your image is to this point, the better. There's room for a fair bit of slop, though.

3 Find your diagonal vanishing point (DVP). The process is pretty much the same as for two-point perspective. Choose a horizon line. Use your straightedge and triangle to find the point on the line you drew in Step 1 or 2 where lines receding to the vanishing points make a right angle. Mark the point (the magic spot). From this point, draw a line 45 degrees between the two receding lines. Where that line meets the horizon is the DVP.

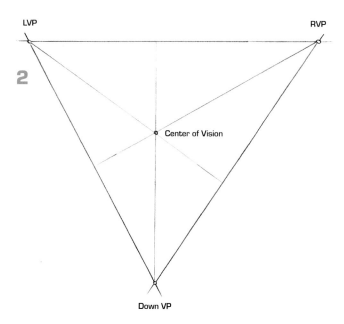

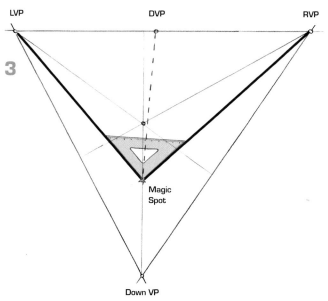

4 Repeat Step 3 for the other two horizons to find the other two DVPs. Keep your lines light to help things from getting too messy and confusing.

5 Put the DVPs into action to draw squares or tile spaces just as you do in one-point and two-point perspective.

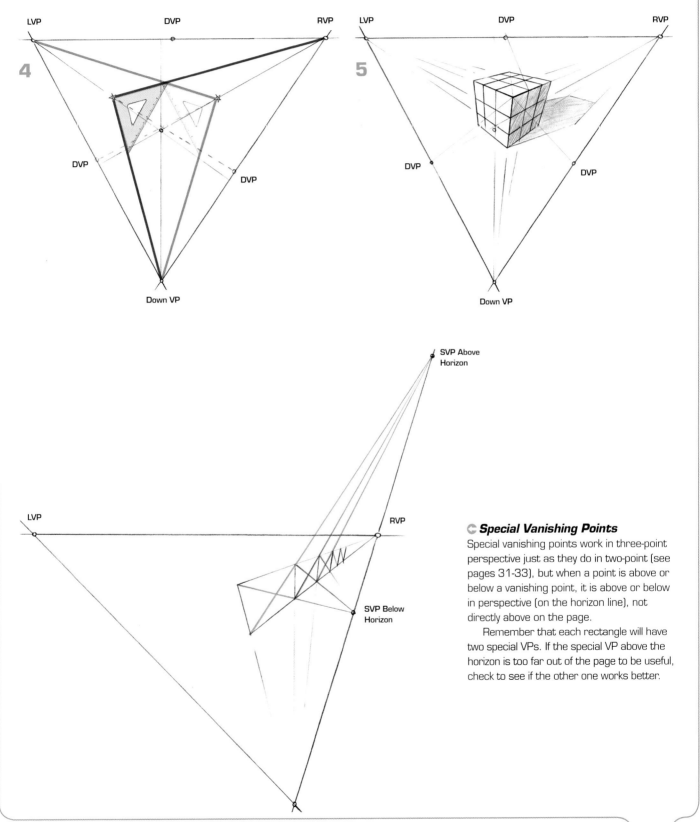

↻ Special Vanishing Points

Special vanishing points work in three-point perspective just as they do in two-point (see pages 31-33), but when a point is above or below a vanishing point, it is above or below in perspective (on the horizon line), not directly above on the page.

Remember that each rectangle will have two special VPs. If the special VP above the horizon is too far out of the page to be useful, check to see if the other one works better.

Use X-Marks-the-Spot in Three-Point

Often we can create a convincing three-point drawing without stopping to place diagonal vanishing points. X-marks-the-spot can divide the face of a building into regular divisions to place windows, etc. Measurements can be moved across forms and through space (for instance to ensure that windows on two sides of a building match each other in size) to build the consistency we need to create believability.

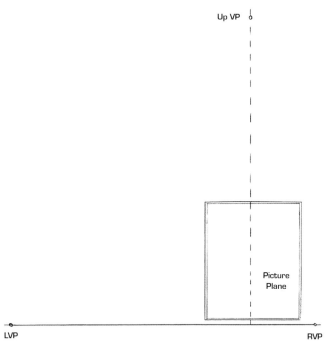

1 In this worm's-eye drawing, place the horizon below the image area. Draw a true vertical line through the center of the picture plane and place the third VP on that line. That will make the "verticals" in the center of the drawing pretty much vertical, with the verticals leaning farther and farther out as you get to the edge of the image. Your sense of up and down gets screwy if you place the drawing too far off that true vertical line.

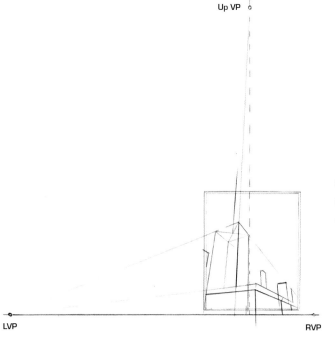

2 Lay in the basic boxes of the tower and the other buildings. The tower roof lines will be at some complicated angles, but we don't need to find vanishing points for them. Use X-marks-the-spot (page 20) to find the center of the top of the tower and draw a vertical receding line up from there.

3 Connect the corners of the base of the roof to a point on the receding vertical line to draw the sloping roof. Pull lines from the center of the *X* to the left and right VPs to move that center division from the top of the tower box to the sides, and then use the vertical (up) VP to draw center lines down from that division. Now you've divided the visible faces of the box neatly in half.

Eyeball a width for the windows on the near side of the box. Move those width measurements up around the top of the box using the right-hand VP (see page 21), and note the points where they cross the diagonal from the X-marks-the-spot in Step 2. Now use the left-hand VP to extend lines through those intersections across the top of the box and down the other visible face of the box. You now have the same window-width measurement on both faces of the tower.

LVP

RVP

Up VP ○

4 Use X-marks-the-spot (page 20) to create consistent heights for the windows on the near side of the tower. Move those measurements sideways along the face and around to the other side. Work out any details you need on the other buildings.

Sketch a person right against one of the windows to get a good figure size proportional to the tower. Move the measurement for the figure sideways in space and draw a new "phantom" figure floating out in space.

LVP

RVP

5 Enlarge the image area of the drawing on a photocopier if you need to. Lay in the shapes for the explosion. Draw a simple curving shape to start the leaping figure, to help give it "sweep" and keep it from being stiff. Use the "phantom" figure as a reference for size to draw the figure.

6 As you begin to render the forms, keep in mind that the components of the tower, the bricks, the shingles and the window hardware all recede to the vanishing points.

7 Finish your rendering. Use all the tools at your disposal to enhance the feeling of depth. Use thicker, bolder line work in the foreground, thinner and simpler line work in the distance. Use the dark, cool color of the sky against the brighter, warm colors of the tower and explosion to help them pop forward. Use more intense colors for the objects closest to you, and slightly grayer colors and less contrast in the distance.

The Tower

Rotated Objects

Rotating objects in three-point perspective is the same as in two-point, it's just easier to get confused because there are more lines. Again, the key is the magic spot you use to find the diagonal vanishing point, where the receding lines meet at right angles (90 degrees) on the line perpendicular to the horizon. Mark that spot—you can rotate any angles you need off of it. And you can find the magic spot for any of the horizon lines, not just the one that represents the real horizon.

For this demonstration, there's an extra long-shot establishing the scene at the imperial palace. It's a grand scene, setting the mood for the action to follow. While the palace is laid out in rectangles, some architectural elements, like the watchtowers, are rotated 45 degrees to the other buildings, simply to make things visually interesting. (The principles here would work for any angle of rotation, 45 degrees just complements the symmetry of the palace design.)

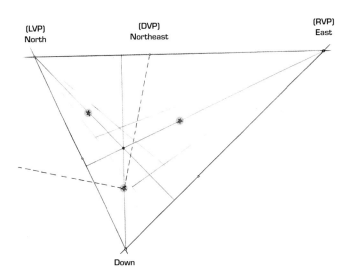

1 Create your horizon triangle, and lay in the perpendicular lines and diagonal vanishing points as described on page 46. Mark all three magic spots (one for each horizon). The magic spots are marked with stars in this example.

Now lay in the first new vanishing point for the rotated object. In this case the rotated objects will stand straight up, but it needs to be an even 45 degrees from the rest of the scene, so place the first new vanishing point right on the diagonal vanishing point on the top horizon. Just like two-point, draw a line from the new VP to the magic spot, and use your triangle to draw a line perpendicular to that line. Where that line meets the horizon is the second VP of the pair.

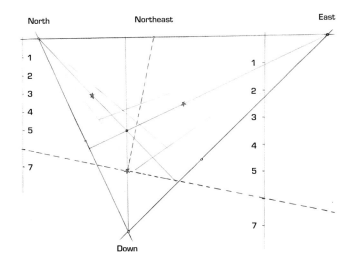

2 Oops! Our paper isn't big enough to fit the intersection of the horizon and that line. This is a common problem in perspective drawing, and we'll bring out a handy trick to beat it. Extend the line perpendicular to your new vanishing point all the way across the page. By trial and error find two places where a vertical line stretched from the horizon to that line measures the same number of units. Note: The number of units is the same, but the units themselves are different. One may be inches and the other could be half-inches or centimeters. In this example, the line on the left is 12cm, and the line on the right is 18cm, or six units of 2cm and six units of 3cm. Measure out the units with little tick marks, 0 being the horizon, 6 being the line in question, and one more pair for good measure.

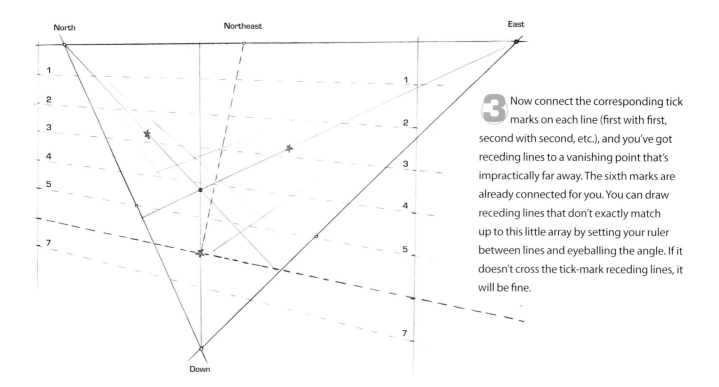

3 Now connect the corresponding tick marks on each line (first with first, second with second, etc.), and you've got receding lines to a vanishing point that's impractically far away. The sixth marks are already connected for you. You can draw receding lines that don't exactly match up to this little array by setting your ruler between lines and eyeballing the angle. If it doesn't cross the tick-mark receding lines, it will be fine.

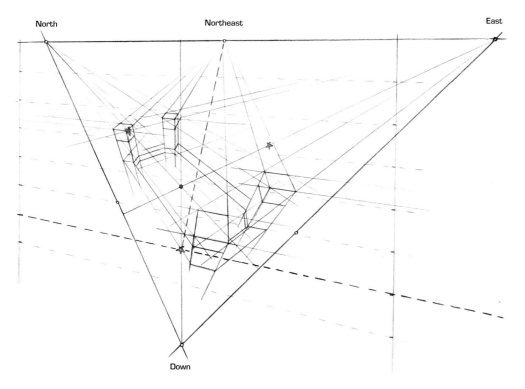

4 Lay in the basic structures of the towers using the new VPs and the down VP. Use the horizon's primary VPs to line up the towers with each other—only their structure is rotated, not their placement.

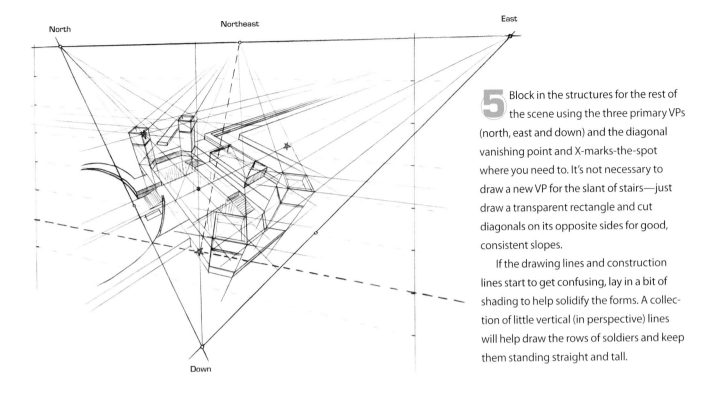

North   Northeast   East

Down

5 Block in the structures for the rest of the scene using the three primary VPs (north, east and down) and the diagonal vanishing point and X-marks-the-spot where you need to. It's not necessary to draw a new VP for the slant of stairs—just draw a transparent rectangle and cut diagonals on its opposite sides for good, consistent slopes.

If the drawing lines and construction lines start to get confusing, lay in a bit of shading to help solidify the forms. A collection of little vertical (in perspective) lines will help draw the rows of soldiers and keep them standing straight and tall.

6 Blow up the image area on a photocopier if you need to. Add detail and render the scene. Just like director Alfred Hitchcock had the house in *Psycho* built a little under size to make Anthony Perkins seem large and slightly odd, we can cheat where we want to. Draw the lookout guard in the nearest tower a little larger than the other guards (and relative to the tower) to emphasize his importance in the scene.

Imperial Palace

perspective mix and match

It's fairly easy to rotate an object (such as a lookout tower in *The Imperial Palace* illustration, page 53, or the cars in the *Power Monkey* illustration, page 41) on one axis, but it gets more involved if you have to rotate it on two or three axes, and the magic spot just isn't up to the task. Maybe you've got to draw a car not just turning a corner, but getting flipped up into the air. You still want it to look good relative to the street scene around it.

As always, a lot of the time you can wing it and have the final drawing come out just fine.

↻ Winging It for a One-Point Perspective Within a Three-Point
A one-point horizon passes through the center of vision, and the vanishing point is right on the three-point's center of vision.

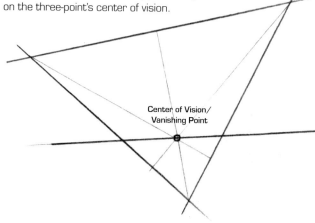

Center of Vision/
Vanishing Point

↻ Winging It for a Two-Point Perspective Within a Three-Point
A two-point horizon passes through the center of vision. Ballpark how far apart vanishing points should be by looking at how far apart the three-point VPs are. They should be a little closer than the average for the three-point VPs.

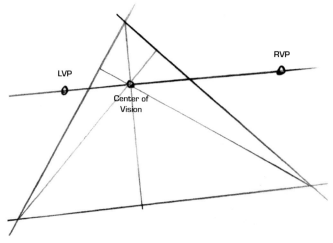

LVP

RVP

Center of
Vision

↻ Winging It for Two Three-Point Perspectives
Using overlays, draw two three-point triangles of roughly the same size. You can even use the same triangle twice, just flipped and rotated. Put them together, matching up the centers of vision. Now you've got two full three-point-perspective systems that match each other pretty well. You could use one set of VPs to draw streets and buildings and cars going in the right direction, and the other VPs to draw a car that's being flipped into the air towards the camera.

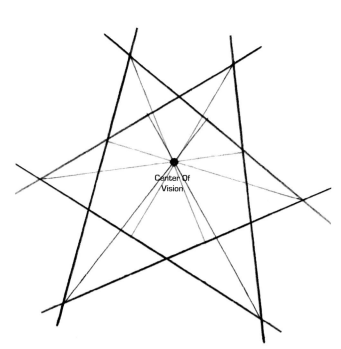

Center Of
Vision

Winging it may not come out right, or it might take a few tries to get it to work correctly. Usually on a complicated drawing, the time you spend trial-and-erroring will probably be just as long as the time it would take to get out the compass and do it by the numbers. It's complicated, but when you break it down into steps, none of the steps are actually difficult, and sometimes it's the only way to get the accuracy you need for that special image.

The cone of vision represents an imaginary cone in real life, with it's point at the eye or the camera lens, but on the picture plane it's represented by a circle.

The cone of vision marks out a space that is a set number of degrees from the center of vision. In a 90-degree cone of vision, if the center of vision is north, then the circle of the cone of vision will mark out every spot 45 degrees away from north: northeast, northwest, a 45-degree slope upwards, a 45-degree slope downwards, and everything rotating between those spots.

Some artists use a 60-degree cone of vision to mark out the distortion-free area of a drawing. If you keep your image area within the confines of that 60-degree cone, you don't have to worry about objects and angles looking wonky. But a 90-degree cone of vision is much cooler. It doesn't just help you map out the safe area of an image, it lets you mix and match an infinite number of perspective systems into a single drawing, all visually consistent with each other.

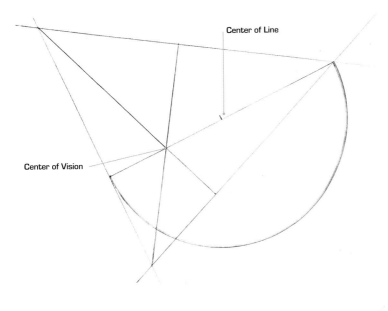

Center of Line

Center of Vision

How to Draw the 90-Degree Cone of Vision

1 Create your three-point triangle and find the center of vision as you would when finding a diagonal vanishing point (see page 46).

Select one of the perpendicular lines you constructed to find the center of vision (the longest is usually the easiest to work with). Measure to find the center of that line and use your compass to draw a half-circle from that center point, connecting both ends of the line. (Place the point of your compass on the center of the line and the drawing tip on one end of the line.)

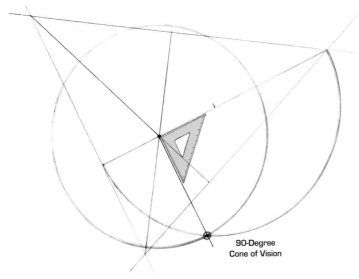

90-Degree Cone of Vision

2 Now draw a line from the center of vision, perpendicular to the line you just built the half-circle around (drawn in red in this example). Where this line crosses the half-circle is a radius of your 90-degree cone of vision. Set your compass point on the center of vision and your drawing tip on this intersection and draw a circle. You've just drawn the 90-degree cone of vision, and all perspectives that agree with this one will have the same 90-degree cone of vision.

Adding Two-Point to Three-Point Perspective

Often your main scene is in standard two-point perspective but has an important object that's rotated to where it's not facing up and down, so you need to add in a three-point system. In the car flipping through the air example, the two-point might be the street scene, seen from eye level as if from a passerby's POV, and the three-point would draw the flipping car.

1 Start with your three-point perspective triangle and 90-degree cone of vision. The horizon for the two-point perspective

passes through the center of vision. Draw a line perpendicular to this new horizon, from the center of vision. Your magic spot is where this line crosses the 90-degree cone of vision. Use the magic spot to place your VPs and DVPs (see page 30).

2 Once you've got those VPs placed, all the rules from two-point and three-point stay the same. Remember that any one box will recede back to either the two-point OR the three-point perspective—never both.

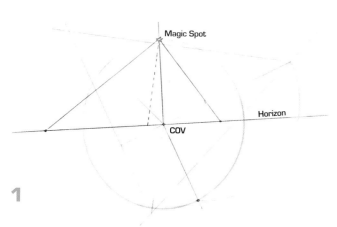

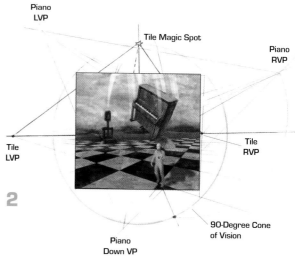

Adding Three-Point to Three-Point Perspective

Now here's where the possibilities become endless. Dozens of cars flipping through the air, countless spaceships swarming around a battle station, dogfighting airplanes, whatever your imagination can dream up. It's a bit trickier than adding two-point to three-point, but none of the individual steps is difficult, so follow the steps, and you can do it.

If you want to avoid some confusion and headache, you can work this out on an overlay. Just draw a new 90-degree cone of vision the same size as the first three-point system's 90-degree cone of vision.

1 Draw a long line through the center of vision. Draw a second line perpendicular to that one, from the center of vision to the edge of the cone of vision circle.

2 Pick a spot on the long line between the center of vision and the edge of the cone of vision. Place the point of your compass on this point, and the drawing tip on the intersection of the cone of vision and the short line of Step 1. Draw a half-circle. Mark the end of this half-circle that falls outside the cone of vision as your first VP.

Draw a perpendicular line through the end of the half-circle that falls within the cone of vision—this is your first horizon line.

3 Place your second vanishing point on the horizon line, preferably just a bit outside the cone of vision. Connect the two vanishing points with a second horizon line and draw a line perpendicular to that horizon line that passes through the center of vision.

4 Mark your third VP at the intersection of that perpendicular line and the first horizon.

You can check your construction by drawing your third horizon line, and making sure that a perpendicular line passes through the center of vision and also through the second VP.

5 Now it's time to get drawing! If you're working on an overlay, put the two three-point triangles together, matching up the centers of vision, and tape them into place. It's a good idea to label the VPs (and DVPs if you're using them) to help prevent confusion. Draw whatever you want, in perfectly matched multiple perspectives. As long as you keep them straight, you can have any number of three-point and two-point perspective systems living in harmony. This illustration has a separate three-point system for each die, and a two-point system for the tiled floor.

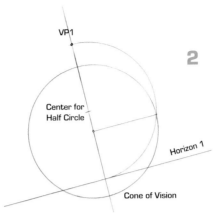

Placing the Center of the Half-Circle

The closer this spot is to the center of vision, the more regular the resulting three-point triangle will be (all three vanishing points roughly the same distance from the center of vision). The closer you place it to the cone of vision, the more extreme the triangle (one VP very far from the center of vision relative to the other two).

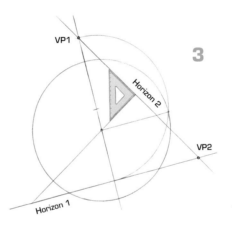

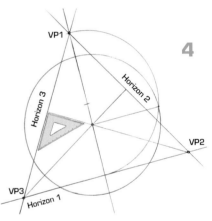

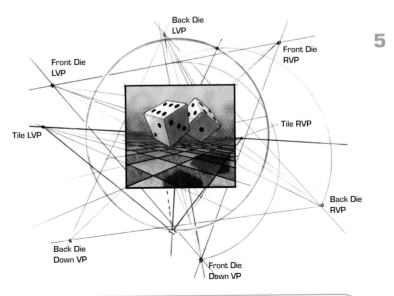

CHAPTER FIVE

DON'T BE A SQUARE

There are a lot of things that

don't simplify into boxes very well, and you've still got to draw them in convincing perspective if you're going to fill out your scene. Cylinders, circles and (gasp) people all obey the laws of perspective.

As you've drawn boxes and rectangles in perspective, your mind has learned how to envision objects in space and see how they translate to a two-dimensional picture plane. This is the ability that will make drawing all these irregular, complicated, rounded or organic forms come together.

Drawing people twisting in space as they fall or jump or fly from extreme angles of view—this is the fun and freedom you want in your drawing.

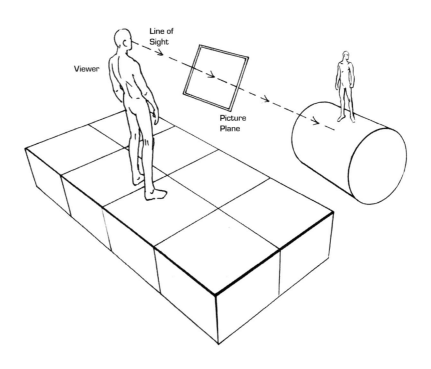

Viewer

Line of Sight

Picture Plane

A circle parallel to the picture plane is still a circle, but as soon as you tilt it into perspective, you get an ellipse.

The ellipse is a strange beast in the world of perspective. Outline a single square floating in perspective, and it's easy to tell which edge is closest. Not so with an outlined circle. The ellipse is symmetrical left to right *and* top to bottom, so you can't tell which edge is closest from the ellipse itself.

There are a number of ways to draw ellipses. One of the most efficient ways is to use an ellipse template from an art/drafting store, but you still need to know a good bit about how ellipses work before you'll know which ellipse on the template to use. Plus, templates never have every single ellipse you'll need or want.

Using the Box Method

The box method is the simplest way to draw ellipses, and the one that takes the most practice. But it's practice well spent that will pay off in speed and in accuracy. Fill a few pages with these ellipses and check them against your templates for accuracy to help your eye learn when an ellipse is true, and when it's collapsed into a football or swollen into a lozenge.

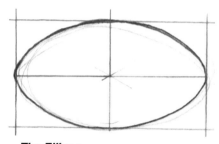

The Ellipse

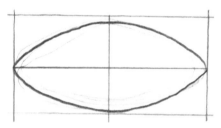

The Football

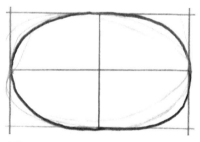

The Lozenge

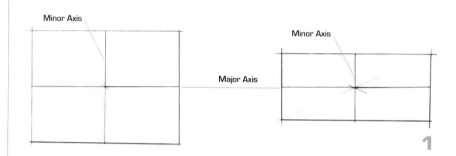

1

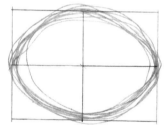

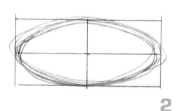

2

1 The first step to drawing a circle in perspective is drawing a rectangle that's not in perspective. Draw a rectangle, and divide it into quarters. The long center line will be the ellipse's major axis, and the short center line will be its minor axis (we'll need to know this in order to properly place these ellipses in drawings). Ellipses are symmetrical around both axes.

2 Quickly and lightly draw a continuous stream of ellipses, swirling around the rectangle. Get the heel of your hand up off the paper and move your hand from your elbow and shoulder rather than just your moving fingers.

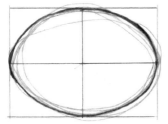

3 Keep a gentle sweep everywhere—ellipses never change direction suddenly, they constantly curve. Rotate the page so it matches the natural curvature of your hand (if you're right-handed, the top left corner of the ellipse will be the easiest to draw, the bottom right the hardest). Let your eye select from all the searching arcs of Step 2 to find and carve out the right line for the ellipse. That's it! The rest is just practice.

3

Inscribing a Circle in a Square

A perfect circle fits inside a perfect square, touching each side at its midpoint. So when you tilt a perfect square in perspective, an ellipse should touch in the same spots. But there are some pitfalls to watch out for.

Note that the center of the ellipse is not the same as the center of the circle it's representing, or the square it's drawn in. Since ellipses are perfectly symmetrical, the center of the ellipse will be closer to the viewer than the center of the circle and square.

The curve of the ellipse will cross the square's diagonals about one-third of the way in from the corner to the center.

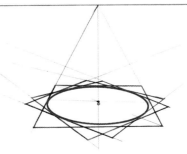

⌒ The Fit Doesn't Change
When drawing ellipses inside squares in perspective, it's helpful to remember that a circle fits in a square the same no matter how you rotate the square.

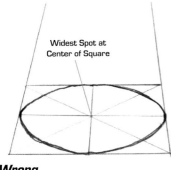

Widest Spot at Center of Square

Wrong

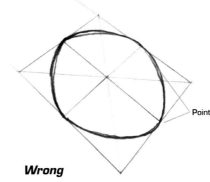

Points

Wrong

Widest Spot at Center of Ellipse.

Correct

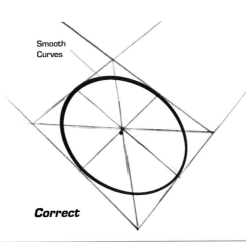

Smooth Curves

Correct

ellipses and cylinders

The most common place we see circles is at the end of cylinders. But ellipses aren't just at the end of the cylinder—the cylinder is made up of an infinite stack of ellipses. The angles of the ellipses (how fat or thin they are) change based on where they are located in space. On templates, the angles of the ellipses are measured in degrees. A 45-degree ellipse represents a circle seen from a 45-degree angle. A 0-degree ellipse is a line. A 90-degree ellipse is a circle.

If a cylinder is vertical, the ellipse that is at the horizon will be collapsed into a straight line. As the cylinder moves away from the horizon (in both directions) the cylinder's ellipses gradually open up, getting closer and closer to becoming circles. (Take your drawing out too far to where it distorts severely and the ellipses start stretching out in the wrong direction.)

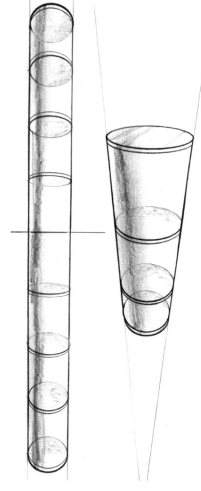

↻ Use Ellipses to Create Cylinders
Cylinders at an angle to the picture plane are also composed of an infinite stack of ellipses, each one of a different angle. Contrary to what your first guess might be, though, the ellipses don't get fatter as the cylinder gets nearer the picture plane, they get thinner. The ellipses are the fattest at the end of the cylinder farther from the picture plane—the narrow end. Remember, skinny ellipses at the wide end, fat ellipses at the narrow end.

How to Draw the Correct Ellipse
Aligned: A popular way to figure out what ellipse to draw at the end of a cylinder is to line up (or *align*) the minor axis of the ellipse with the center line of the cylinder. This is strictly true only at the horizon or vertically on the center of vision, but it looks pretty good, and is a lot easier and faster than other methods. Sometimes it even looks better than working out the "right" ellipse, so use it judiciously.

Inscribed: Sometimes, though, especially in complicated drawings where the ellipses will be visually compared to a lot of boxes in the scene, you need a more accurate angle for the ellipse. To do this, *inscribe* the ellipse in a square. Draw the square, divide it in half in both directions, draw the diagonals, and mark one-third in along each diagonal. Now draw in an ellipse that touches each side of the square at its middle, and passes through the diagonals at those one-third marks. You won't need to draw the major and minor axes of the ellipse at all.

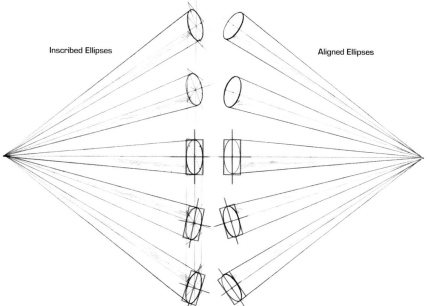

Inscribed Ellipses   Aligned Ellipses

◯ Aligned vs. Inscribed Ellipses
Close to the horizon, it's difficult to tell which ellipse was drawn using alignment and which was inscribed in a square. But, the farther away from the horizon the cylinders get, the more notable the difference in the rotation of the axes (marked in red) of the ellipses.

Cylinders in Space

Often, we wind up drawing a long skinny box that's square on its little end to create a cylinder, keeping in mind the cylinder will be notably narrower than the box that was used to construct it. This lets you find the center of the circle (not needed to draw the ellipse itself, but frequently useful in drawing the object using the ellipse [e.g., placing the hole in the center of a CD in the right place]).

Since ellipses fit in squares, it's often handy to lay in the diagonal vanishing point in your scene to get the proportions right.

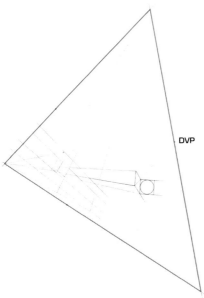

DVP

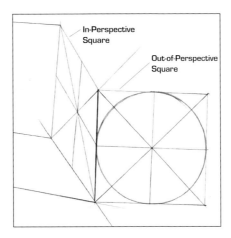

In-Perspective Square

Out-of-Perspective Square

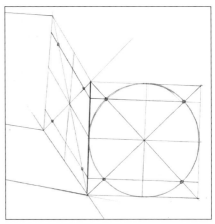

1 Inside your three-point perspective triangle, lay in the basic shapes of a space station. Use the diagonal vanishing point to make the box's end a true square. For a little help with the ellipse, rotate the end square out of perspective like a box top. It's easy to do—pick a side of the square (pick one of the larger ones to make it easier on yourself), measure that side and draw a new square using that side—not a square in perspective, but a plain, old, flat-on-the-paper square using a ruler and a triangle. Use a compass or a circle template to draw a circle inside the square.

2 This is a closer look at the circle from Step 1. Divide both squares (the in-perspective one and the out-of-perspective one) into quadrants using X-marks-the-spot. The circle meets the square at those midway lines and now you can see where the circle crosses the diagonal lines.

3 Draw parallel lines down the out-of-perspective square starting at the intersection of the circle and the diagonal lines, and going down to the side common to the two squares. Now use receding lines to the vanishing point to move those measuring lines forward across the in-perspective square. Note where they cross the diagonal lines of the in-perspective square.

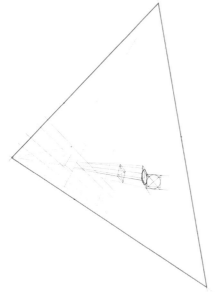
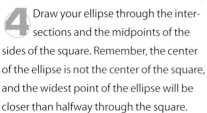
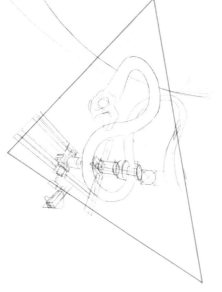
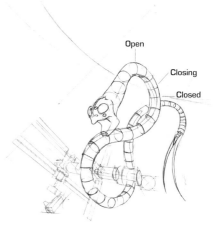

Open
Closing
Closed

4 Draw your ellipse through the intersections and the midpoints of the sides of the square. Remember, the center of the ellipse is not the center of the square, and the widest point of the ellipse will be closer than halfway through the square.

Move those measuring lines down the long rectangle, and pull them back to the VP anywhere else you want to draw another ellipse.

5 Use the ellipses you've drawn to create the cylinders for the space station. Lay in the giant serpent, thinking about the twists and turns it makes through space. Lay in the tiny spaceship—it's so little and unconnected to the rest of the space that you can wing the perspective on it.

6 Find the ellipses that make up the serpent—it's not straight, but it's still a cylinder and the ellipses will help give it volume. Start out with those parts of the turns where it changes between moving away from the camera and moving towards the camera—place a 0-degree ellipse (straight line!) there, and then work outward, tracking where ellipses open up and thin back down.

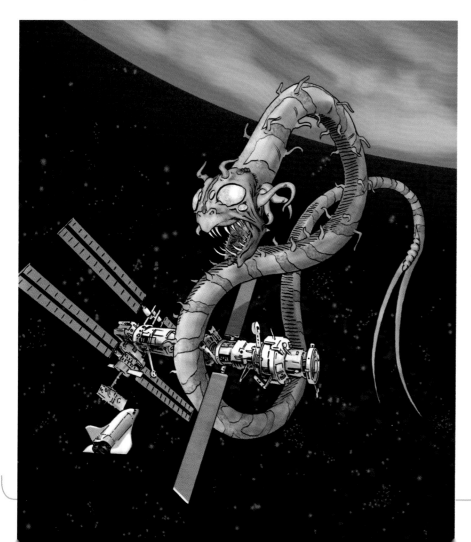

7 When you render the scene, keep in mind the ellipses of the serpent and how they affect the structure and any surface details. In a space scene like this, we're used to vast expanses of vision. If we drew a city scene with the vanishing points this close in it would look pretty distorted, but the lonely shape of the station looks just fine.

When you're drawing figures in perspective, you need to draw the volume of the complicated forms of the human figure, not just the outline. Do this by keeping in mind the cross sections of the body.

Diagram View

This diagram shows cross sections of various points in the figure. On the diagram, the lines that wrap around the cross sections all look like straight lines. You see the top of the head head-on, the bottom of the feet head-on, and everything in between head on. That's what makes it a diagram. You'll never see this in a comic drawing.

Let's take a look at the vertical (standing) figure. There's only one point in the figure where you'll see the cross section as a straight line—at the horizon. The farther you move from the horizon, the more the cross sections open up.

Chest-Height View

When the eye level (and therefore the horizon) is at chest height, the band around the cross section at the figure's chest is a straight line. Up at his crown, you see a bit of the cross section opening up. At his midsection you see the cross sections opening up in the other direction, and the farther down you go, the more of the cross sections we see.

Below-the-Horizon View

When drawing a figure completely below the horizon, you see all cross sections open, but not open the same amount. Just like the cylinder, the cross sections closest to the viewer will be the narrowest, those farthest away will be the widest.

Ankle-Height View

When the eye level is at the ankles, the cross sections below the knees are slightly opened to you, and the cross sections get further and further open until you almost see the full cross section at the crown.

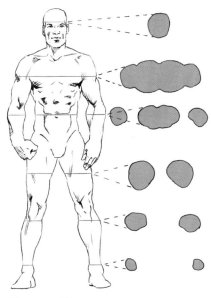

Diagram View

Chest-Height View

Below-the-Horizon View

Ankle-Height View

Drawing Clothing

Clothing, particularly hat bands, belts, gloves, and that sort of thing, wrap around the figure just as these cross section lines do, straighter towards the horizon, more full farther from the horizon.

If you're drawing a figure from an unusual angle, sometimes you need a little help to get everything placed in perspective. Building the figure out of rectangles and cylinders is possible, but more trouble than it's worth, and usually winds up with a very stiff and unnatural result.

Receding lines aren't much help in drawing the complicated structures of the human figure, but they are very useful in lining up paired spots like knees, elbows and eyes. "Vertical" receding lines help you find "up" in relation to the figure and also track how much the figure visually shrinks as it moves away from the viewer in space.

With complicated forms in perspective, even though you're not building forms with the receding lines, it's helpful to suspend the form within a perspective grid. With the case of the standing figure, you can help yourself out by putting some regular divisions in. Divide the standing space of the figure into quarters and you can sketch in the silhouette/diagram of the figure with the chest level at the first division, just below the center of the hips on the middle, and just below the knees on the third.

With the guide in place, draw the figure by floating it into the grid, filling out in front and behind the diagram/silhouette. Keep in mind how the cross sections open up and affect the outline of the interlocking forms of the figure.

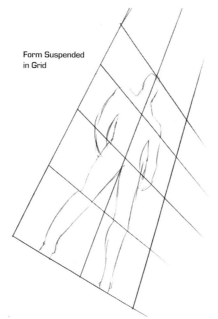

Form Suspended in Grid

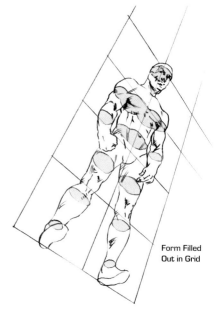

Form Filled Out in Grid

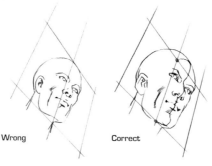

Wrong

Correct

When placing the foreshortened figure into measured spaces like this, remember that the forms fit into the space in perspective, not the space on the paper. The measuring lines should touch the top of the head and the level of the chin in space, not the top and bottom of the drawing of the head.

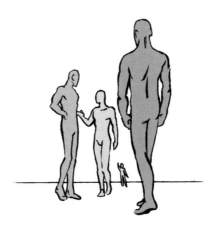

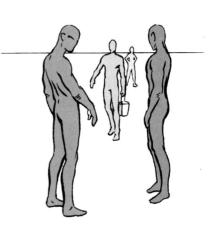

Figures on the Horizon

The horizon will pass through figures of the same height at the same point. This is often the only thing you need to know to draw groupings of figures. So if the horizon crosses one figure at the neck, it will cross all of them there (with allowances for height differences). And, if it crosses one figure at the ankles, it will cross all of them there.

☞ Gesturing Limbs

A limb parallel to the picture plane has its cross sections seen side-on as straight lines. As the limb starts to point at the camera, the cross sections open up and get closer to each other on the page. Eventually the limb becomes drawn as a series of overlapping circles.

Using the Ground Plane as the Bottom Panel Border

Some artists (including some *very* good ones) like to make the horizon line the ground plane and draw that line as the bottom panel border. To my eye, grounding the foreground and background figures to the same bold panel border line damages the sense of depth—plus I always start thinking about where the viewer would have to be to see that shot.

☞ Ellipses and Cross Sections

Drawing accurate cross sections is usually not necessary. Simplifying the cross section to a circle is much faster and does what you need it to do. A few well-placed ellipses can be the key to making sense of complicated poses as you draw them.

What parts of the figure are coming towards the camera? What parts are moving away? Remember that these limbs will have their cross sections open up, and the limb itself will shorten on the page. What parts (if any) are parallel to the picture plane and so have flat ellipses and don't foreshorten at all?

complex curves

How to Draw a Car

In the past, perspective books instructed artists to draw cars by making a small cereal box lying on top of a big cereal box. When the Mercury Grand Marquis was king of the road, this was fairly true. These days, most cars bend and curve from every angle and to make them out of boxes really isn't worth the trouble.

But cars still obey the laws of perspective because they are symmetrical. More importantly, since they're so familiar, they won't look right unless you draw them in proper perspective.

When drawing a complicated form like a car, it's good to start out with a lightly drawn perspective web/grid. There's no need to measure out the lines, just draw a bunch of them to help give a sense of space. You're not going to draw the car in with the lines, you're going to suspend the car in the perspective web/grid.

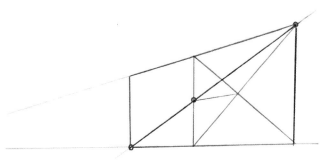

⋒ *Doubling Space*

When drawing symmetrical objects like cars, it's handy to double a shape in perspective. Doubling space is simply the flip side of the X-marks-the-spot dividing space trick, and it uses the same principle. Take the rectangle you want to double and extend the sides in the direction you want to draw the new rectangle.

Find the center of the original rectangle (using X-marks-the-spot). Draw a line in perspective from the center over to the side that will be shared between the original rectangle and its copy to find its center point.

From a far corner of the original rectangle, draw a line that passes through the center point of the common side. Where this new line crosses the extended sides, draw the final line of the new rectangle. Simple, huh? And pretty powerful when you put it in action.

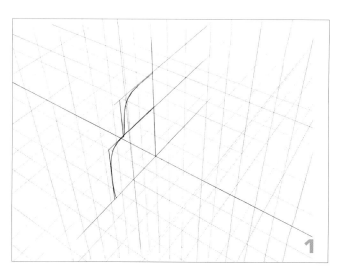

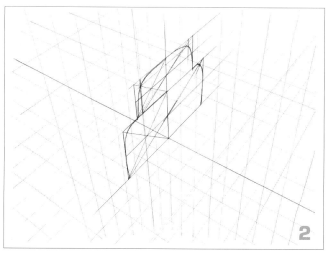

1 Lay in the center axis of the car, at its base, and a vertical line near its center.

Draw in one half of a cross section of the car, and extend the lines of it horizontally. Depending on which cross section you've chosen to start with, it's usually pretty much the front view of the car.

2 Double the space to lay in the other half of the cross section. If you need more than the basic rectangle shape, you can draw in an interior rectangle with its corner on the curve, and double the space again to locate the same point on the curve to the other side. Often you can just lay in the diagonal on both sides of the center, and draw a line across where the curve crosses the diagonal to locate where the curve crosses the other side's diagonal.

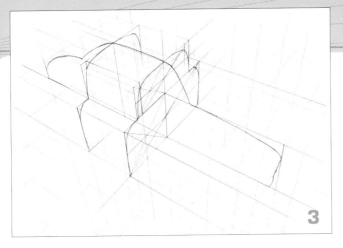

3

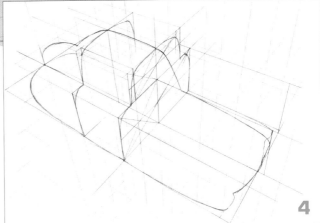

4

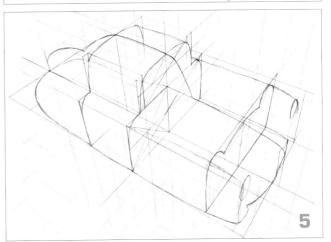

5

3 If the cross section you've drawn is duplicated anywhere, use the grid to move it along the center line to draw a copy of it. Draw in the perpendicular cross section (pretty much the side view) at the center line of the car.

4 Lay in the near half of the "footprint" of the car—basically its top view—on the base plane.

5 Double the space to draw the far half of the footprint. Draw in any other cross sections you need to finish up the volume of the space.

6 Now you've got enough information to connect the cross sections and find exterior contours (the silhouette) of the car and any other information you need. For the wheels you can lay in squares where the wheels will be, mark thirds in on the diagonals, and draw in the ellipses (correct way) or just draw a line for the axles, and match it up to the minor axis on the ellipse template (easy way).

7 You've got the information you need for the structure of the car and the web in place to help you place any symmetrical points and line up any details. Render and detail, and you're done.

This method will let you draw really accurate objects, but there are a lot of obvious places you can cut corners when you don't need that extra accuracy. Think twice before skimping on the initial grid, though—even if you're winging the symmetry and only hinting in one cross section in each direction, that initial grid will anchor the vehicle in the proper space.

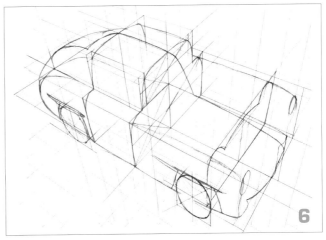

6

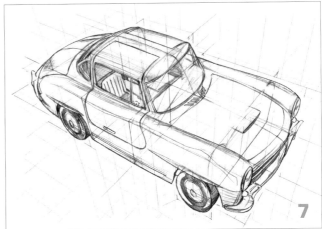

7

Draw a Scene With a Crowd

When dealing with crowds, you can hang figures off the horizon (the horizon crosses every figure at the armpits, that sort of thing), but sometimes you need a bit more to really fill in a scene. Making sure the figures and the buildings around them are proportional to each other is one key to crowd scenes that is often forgotten about until it's too late to easily fix.

This example is drawn in three-point perspective, but since we want to include the horizon in the image area, the third vanishing point has to be a very large distance away. Draw a true vertical through your horizon at the center of your image area. Use measured tick marks on either side to work on the vertical receding lines

(see page 51). If you slide your triangle along the vertical receding lines that pass through the vanishing points, you'll be able to find the center of vision where the perpendicular lines your triangle draws cross the true vertical line you drew through the center of vision. If the center of vision isn't reasonably close to the horizon, you won't be able to include the horizon in the drawing without some serious distortions.

You can move the third vanishing point up (that is, make the distance between the ticks on the top row larger) and try again until the center of vision is where you need it to be.

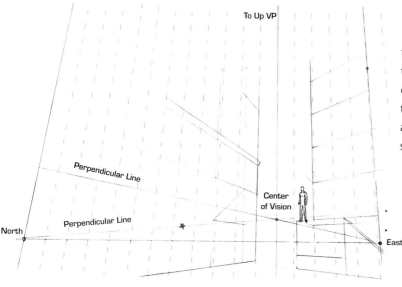

1 When drawing buildings and figures, you need to make sure the figures can fit inside! As you lay in the basic shapes of the buildings, mark off height lines to represent each story of the structure. You can use a diagonal vanishing point across vertical lines to maintain story height, or use the doubling space method to add on each floor. Draw one figure in the scene, making sure he's proportional to the story height.

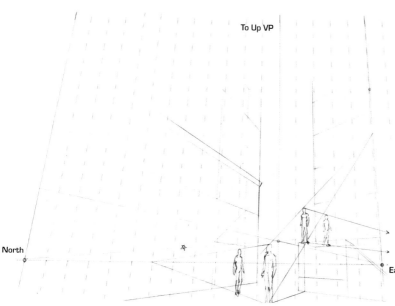

2 To project the first figure down to the level below, trace a line down from his feet to the ground plane, and then forward across the ground using the main vanishing points. Then find a new vanishing point on one of the side horizon lines that connects the first figure's feet with where you want the feet to be on the ground. Draw two receding lines to that spot to mark off the head and foot location of the new figure.

Crowds in Other Perspectives

You can draw crowd scenes in any perspective system. One- and two-point perspective are even easier. Since vertical lines don't recede, you can move figures up and down in space by just measuring figure height with a ruler and drawing another figure directly above or below at the same size.

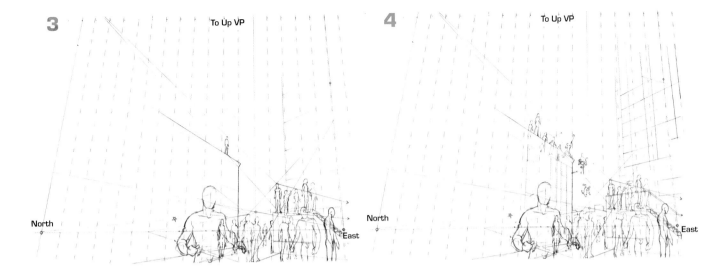

3 Project as many figures as you want. The VP for figures standing on the same level as each other (whether that's ground level, rooftop or subbasement) will be on the bottom horizon. Draw a receding line across the top of the figure's head and another at the bottom of his feet. Draw new figures at other spots within these lines, using vertical receding lines to keep them standing upright within the scene. If foreground figures get too large, project them head to waist rather than head to foot. Project a new figure or two on top of the far building.

4 Project the last group of figures on top of the far building. Project simple standing figures into space, then partly erase them to use them as size reference to draw figures falling (or leaping, swinging or flying) through space.

Zombie Block Party

5 Render your scene! Keep in mind where the horizon is as you draw each figure. Is the viewer looking up at them? A little or a lot? Are the zombies' limbs parallel to the picture plane, or do they point towards or away from the camera? Think of the ellipses and how they are shown in the figures' forms and clothing.

Vanishing Points for Projected Figures

This exercise projects figures on two axes only. The first figure projected was moved both down and west (away from the east VP and away from the up VP) from the original. That puts the projecting VP on the horizon line that connects the east VP and the up VP.

The figures standing on the ground are projected on north and east axes, but not up, so their projecting VPs are on the bottom horizon. Projecting a figure on all three axes (moving it north, east and down all at the same time) puts the projection VP off the horizon lines completely and is almost always more headache than it's worth.

CHAPTER SIX

FIVE-POINT PERSPECTIVE

Five-point perspective is the

simplest of curvilinear perspectives, and the one most frequently used in comic illustration. It's the curvilinear equivalent of one-point perspective, but the wide-open field of view it creates makes it much more flexible than one-point perspective.

When I was first learning to draw in perspective, I quickly grew frustrated by how little I could draw. My eye saw an enormous swath of the room all at once, but straight-line perspective only allowed me to draw the tiniest chunk of the room. It seemed to me that the eye didn't see straight lines as straight at all. When we step up to a wall, we see it tapering away from us on both sides.

People can argue whether the eye actually sees straight lines as curves or not, but one thing's for certain—drawing straight lines as curves opens up the drawing area to an almost limitless extent. It can create the feeling of being up in the very middle of a scene, rather than just in front of it. It also gives the illusion of looking around in a room rather than seeing only one tiny snapshot of one view of the room.

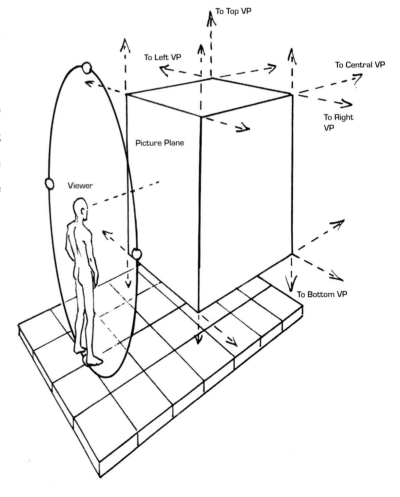

how to draw arcs

Drawing a straight line from a vanishing point is pretty easy; simply slide the ruler up to the vanishing point, point the ruler in the direction you want it to go and drag the pencil down its side.

Drawing consistent curves from vanishing points is a little tougher. For curvilinear perspective, we draw arcs (that's the technical name for little bits of a circle), which requires the use of a compass.

To draw an arc, you need two vanishing points, a line connecting them and a bisecting line (a line that cuts the connecting line in half at a 90-degree angle).

To draw the bisecting line, you could measure it with a ruler, and then use a triangle to draw in the bisecting line, but there's an easier, more accurate way, especially since you have a compass handy.

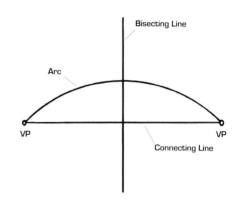

1 Start off with the two vanishing points (the connecting line is usually helpful, but you don't need it). Set your compass to any radius larger than halfway between the two vanishing points. A setting that reaches three-quarters of the way across is usually good. Place the point of the compass on one vanishing point and draw some arcs above and below the connecting line.

2 Without changing the setting of the compass, place the compass point on the other vanishing point and draw two more arcs that intersect the arcs you drew in the last step.

3 Take your straightedge and draw a line through the intersections of the arcs. There's your bisecting line! Make it as long as your paper permits.

4 Now that you've got your vanishing points and bisecting line set up, you can draw almost any arc you need. It's a simple matter of putting the pointy foot of the compass anywhere on the bisecting line, and the drawing point on one of the vanishing points. Draw an arc connecting the two vanishing points and there you go.

The closer your arcs get to the connecting line, the farther out the foot of the compass has to be. If you've got a beam compass, or a compass with a beam exten-

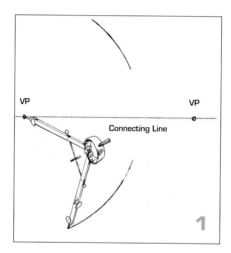

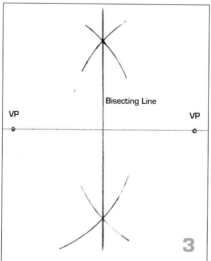

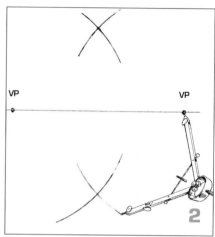

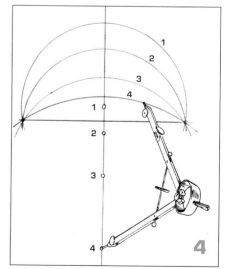

sion, you can go out pretty far and draw arcs quite close to the connecting line.

To draw really big arcs, you sometimes need to move the pointy foot of the compass up above the connecting line, to point 1 for example.

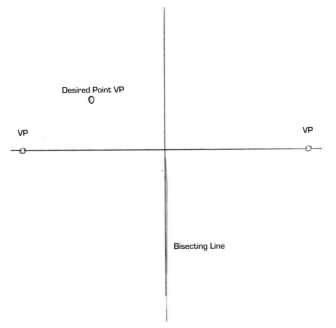

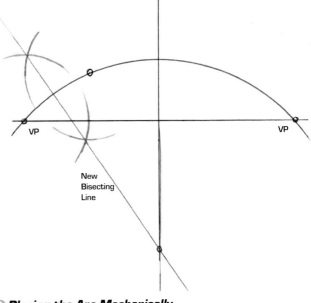

Draw It Where You Want It

Say you're drawing a house. You can't put the line for the top of the roof just anywhere; it has to be in the right spot. Drawing an arc is easy, but drawing exactly the arc you need is more of a challenge. It gets easier with practice.

Placing the Arc Mechanically

There's a mechanical way to find the right arc. Mark the point you want to draw an arc through. Draw a new bisecting line between that point and the vanishing point closer to it. Where that new bisecting line crosses the main bisecting line is where the compass foot needs to go to draw the arc you need.

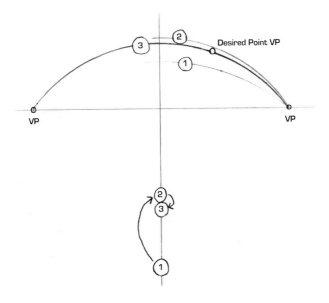

Eyeballing the Arc

There's a simpler way to place the arc, although it may take a few tries. Imagine the bisecting line between the desired point and the near vanishing point, and eyeball where it would cross the main bisecting line. Now put your compass point on that spot, and adjust the drawing tip to hit the vanishing point. Then swing the drawing point over to the desired point to test whether it hits it. You'll usually need a couple of tries. If your arc goes below the desired point (in this example, 1), move the compass point up. Then adjust the compass drawing tip to the vanishing point, and swing it over to check if it hits the point you want.

If the arc goes above the desired point (in this example, 2), move the compass point farther out on the bisecting line. Always adjust the compass to reach the vanishing point first, and then check it to see if it reaches the desired point. You'll quickly zero the compass point in on exactly the right spot (in this example, 3).

draw a box in five-point perspective

There are four vanishing points around the outer circle of the bull's-eye, and a fifth at the center of the circle. Like one-point perspective, the viewer is looking flat-on at the main form.

Usually, this means the central vanishing point represents straight ahead, the top vanishing point "up," the bottom vanishing point "down" and the left and right vanishing points are the viewer's left and right.

In this case the horizontal line of the bull's-eye is the picture's horizon. Or the viewer could be looking straight up or straight down at the object. If the viewer is lying on his/her back, the central vanishing point becomes up, the top vanishing point above the viewer's head, say, north, the bottom south, the left east and the right west.

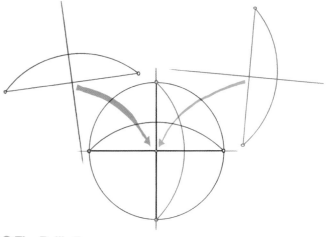

↻ The Bull's-Eye
The framework for five-point perspective is the bull's-eye. It's made up of two vanishing point pairs/bisecting-line frameworks: one turned 90 degrees to the other and stacked on top. This way the connecting line of one vanishing point pair is the bisecting line of the other.

1 Draw one horizontal line crossed by a vertical line. The closer these lines are to a perfect 90-degree angle to each other, the better your drawing will work out. Place the point of the compass at the intersection, and draw a largish circle. Where that circle crosses the lines makes four of the vanishing points. The fifth is right in the center where the horizontal and vertical lines cross.

2 Place the point of the compass on the horizontal line, set the drawing tip to the top vanishing point, and draw an arc down to the bottom vanishing point. Repeat the process for another arc on the opposite side. If you want the box exactly centered, you can keep the same compass setting as you flip it over to the opposite side, but that perfect symmetry can be a bit boring. You might want to make the second side a bit farther in or farther out from center than the first one.

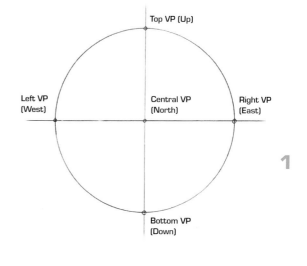

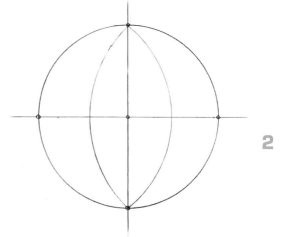

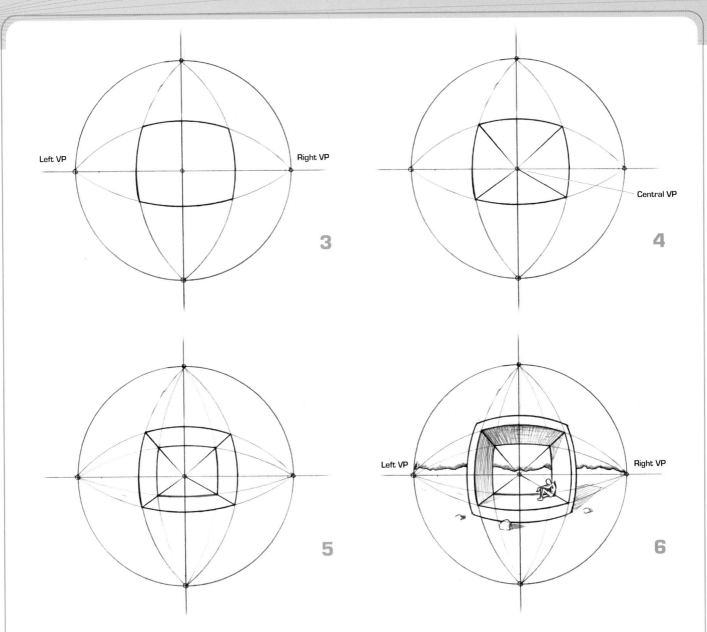

Now place the compass point on the vertical line and the drawing tip on the left or right vanishing point. Draw two more arcs to finish the front face of the box.

Use a straightedge to pull receding lines from the corners of the box back to the central vanishing point.

Draw four more arcs to draw the back face of the box. Since these arcs are closer to the center than the first arcs, the compass point will need to be placed farther out from the circle. The first of these arcs can be pretty arbitrary, but the last three will need to be accurately drawn from the intersections of the first back arc and the receding lines. Draw these accurately by following the steps on page 75, using the intersections as your desired points.

If any of these arcs have to be drawn very close to the connecting line, you may need to set the compass point farther away than is possible. If this is the case, you'll need to freehand that arc, or use a French curve or flexible curve to draw it.

Clean up the box, knocking back any construction lines you don't want, and adding any rendering the box needs to exist in space. Remember that the horizontal line connecting the left and right vanishing point is the scene's horizon.

Measuring space in curvilinear perspective can be a bit of a problem. Our old favorite X-marks-the-spot trick works here theoretically, but you can't draw the X with a straightedge; it needs to be made out of the correct two arcs. Sometimes you can freehand it with reasonable success, but sometimes it's not worth it.

But there is compensation! The coolest little trick in five-point perspective (and four-point for that matter) is this: Equal ticks on the bisecting line draw arcs of equal divisions receding away in space.

The grid with parallel arcs divides space in both directions for the planes receding away from the viewer. But what about dividing the planes that are flat-on to the viewer? There's a neat trick for that, too.

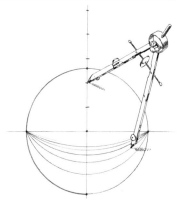

Measuring Space

1 Mark out equal measurements along one of your bisecting lines (the measurements can be whatever size you want—three inches, a centimeter—whatever you choose). Now place the compass point on each of these tick marks, set the drawing tip to a vanishing point and draw out one arc for each tick. Voila! Lovely little parallel arcs receding in space.

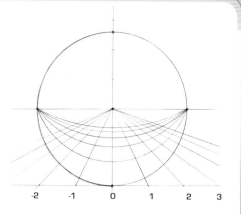

2 Draw a horizontal line touching the bottom of the bull's-eye circle. Measure out equal divisions along the line and pull receding lines back to the central vanishing point from each tick mark. If you want to make a consistent grid with the previous dividing arcs, just measure the space between the nearest arcs at their widest point, and make the measurements on your new line about 1½ times that size.

Diagonal Vanishing Points on the Bull's-Eye Circle

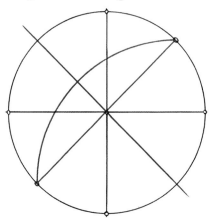

1 Rotating new vanishing points off the outer circle of the bull's-eye is simple. Rotate a new vanishing point pair and bisecting line halfway between the existing vanishing points. This will put the connecting line and bisecting line at 45-degree angles to the bull's-eye's straight lines. If you find it easier, you can use tracing paper to rotate an existing VP pair and bisecting line rather than measuring out new perpendicular lines.

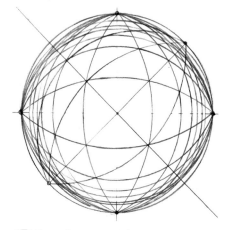

2 From the new vanishing points and bisecting lines, draw diagonal arcs. Use these arcs just as you would diagonal vanishing points in one-, two- and three-point perspective. Draw arcs with the main bull's-eye at the intersections with the diagonal arcs to create a grid.

Rotating Vanishing Point Pairs

You can rotate a new vanishing point pair to any angle, not just 45 degrees. Just turn the vanishing point pair, or a whole second bull's-eye, to wherever you want it, and you can draw rotated shapes at any angle, as long as you're still looking flat-on at their ends.

In the Center of Action

Curvilinear perspective opens up the field of view, but since it's so uncommon, it can also call up all sorts of moods—disorientation, otherworldliness and the like. It's quite literally a shift in perception. Often we pull in a picture plane that's fairly small on the bull's-eye and get the advantages with only a minimal notable curvature to the lines, but sometimes we pull back to include the whole bull's-eye, maybe even more.

Here we want to draw our gravity-bound hero frustrated in her pursuit of a winged monster through the city. The creature could disappear to anywhere, so we want to hint at the expanse of the city. We don't want to have to pull way back from the scene to show the expanse, so we use five-point perspective to put us in the center of the action.

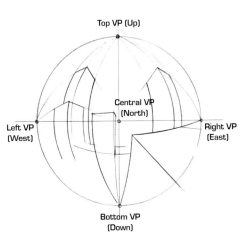

1 Using the bull's-eye, rough in the basic shapes of the buildings. The building closest to the center will be a cathedral with all sorts of symmetrical things about it, so roughly lay that in, knowing it will change.

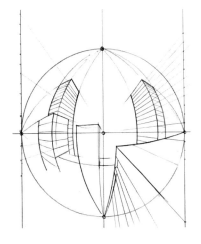

2 To mark off story heights on the sky-scrapers, draw vertical lines touching the sides of the circle. Mark off equal ticks on those lines for each building. You can use horizontal arcs to connect the buildings to make the story heights match up, or more likely just wing it. If the building is a little farther away, the ticks are a little closer together. Pull receding lines off those tick marks to the central vanishing point. Draw arcs between the left and right vanishing point pair to continue the story divisions across the front faces of the buildings.

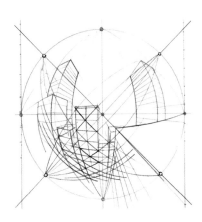

3 Time for our diagonal vanishing point pair! Let's use a whole new diagonal bull's-eye. Draw a grid with it (and any horizontal or vertical arcs you need from the main bull's-eye) to cover the face of the cathedral. Use that grid to build the symmetrical shape of the cathedral, find midpoints on its towers and mark off story heights.

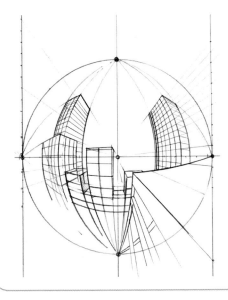

4 The diagonal arcs can also be used to find verticals across the front faces of the other buildings. Where a diagonal arc crosses the story height divisions, draw vertical arcs. Vertical divisions on the receding faces of the buildings can be laid in using the equal ticks on the bisecting line trick (see page 78). Find the point on the horizontal bisecting line that draws one edge of the building in question and measure off equal ticks from that point.

5 Draw in the top faces of the cathedral's towers and use the divisions on the face of the cathedral, and a little bit of just eyeballing it, to place the center of each tower top.

Pull vertical arcs up from the center of each tower for the center of the tower spires. Now it's a matter of connecting that top point to the four corners of the tower top beneath it. There's not much to be gained by trying to find vanishing point pairs and bisecting lines for each one, so just grab your French curve (or just free-hand) to lay in arcs to connect the dots. The closer to the center VP you get, the closer to straight the arcs should be.

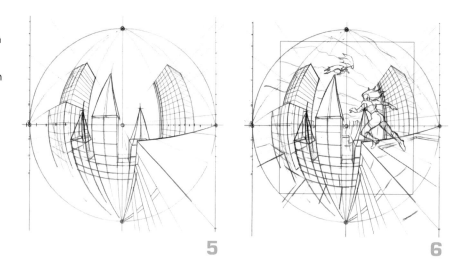

6 Placing figures in curvilinear perspective can be a special challenge. Sometimes we want to draw them in strict accordance to the perspective, but sometimes that gives a distorted feel you don't want. Since the figure here is near the horizon, her distortion won't be too severe. Striking a compromise between a figure drawn in strict accordance and one drawn straight up makes the scene more dynamic and makes her stand out, without taking it so far that she doesn't look like part of the picture. You can also avoid perspective problems by making the character lean forward. If she were standing up straight, she would either have to conform to the curvature of the vertical building behind her or jarringly break with it. Once everything is in place, decide where you want your panel borders to be.

7 Render the scene and bring it to life! Keep an eye on the web of lines you've built up to help keep your details (and your brushstrokes or texture marks) reinforcing the form.

Elusive Prey

Oftentimes the equal tick tricks can do the same job of a diagonal vanishing point on the horizon rather than on the bull's-eye circle, but sometimes you need a diagonal vanishing point! Don't worry, finding one is a breeze.

1 In your bull's-eye, mark in a diagonal vanishing point on the horizon line exactly halfway between the circle and the center. Now, on the opposite side of the circle, make a mark exactly three-quarters of the way from the center of the circle to its edge. Draw a vertical line through that point—this is your diagonal bisecting line.

The second vanishing point (there's always a pair) is off to the side of the picture, but there's no point in drawing it in. One point and a bisecting line are all you need to draw your arcs.

2 Place the compass point on the new diagonal bisecting line and the drawing tip on the diagonal vanishing point. Then start drawing diagonal lines all over the place. Ground, ceiling, through space, anywhere. You can use them to construct grids on the ground plane as usual.

If you want a diagonal vanishing point that draws lines on walls instead of floors or ceilings, take the two steps above and rotate the action 90 degrees so that the DVP is on the vertical line of the bull's-eye, and the diagonal bisecting line is horizontal.

Try DVPs to Render the Main Object

You can use a pair of diagonal vanishing points to render your main objects, treating them as the primary VPs and the central VP as the DVP. This gives you a new space that's got a little something extra from your basic five-point. The cover of this book was drawn using this technique.

Remember how you can rotate a new bull's-eye around the center of the first? You can combine that trick with this method for placing diagonal vanishing points to place new vanishing points that are neither on the bull's-eye circle nor on its connecting lines.

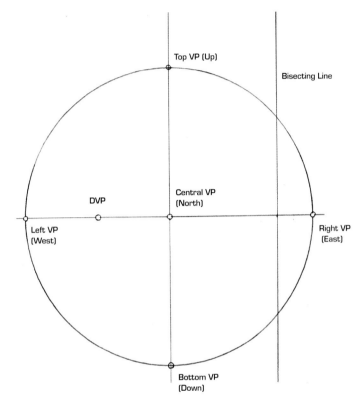

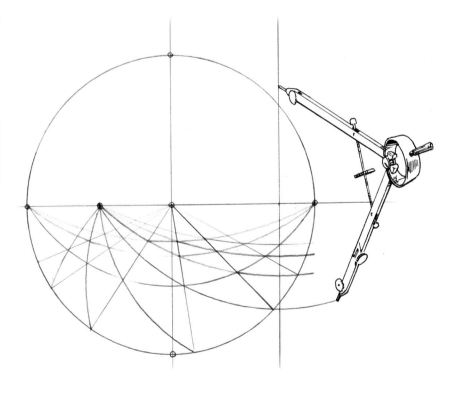

Draw a Scene in Five-Point Perspective

Let's draw a good establishing shot for a castle in a science fiction/ fantasy realm and have the main characters running up the stairs. Five-point perspective is good for the otherworldly nature, but with all the stairs and railings, we'll need to draw a lot of arcs that don't converge on any of the five points of the bull's-eye.

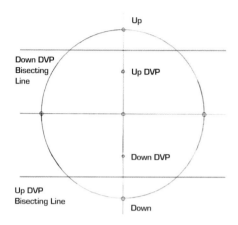

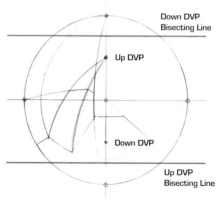

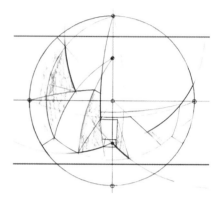

1 To make life easy, draw the staircases at 45-degree angles. Start with your bull's-eye and add a diagonal vanishing point halfway between the central vanishing point and the top vanishing point. Put its bisecting line three-fourths of the way between the central vanishing point and the bottom vanishing point.

Place a second diagonal vanishing point between the central and bottom vanishing point, and draw its bisecting line three-fourths of the way from the central to the top vanishing point.

2 Draw in the basic shape of the first staircase, placing your compass foot on the up bisecting line and drawing arcs from the up diagonal vanishing point. Use the bull's-eye to complete the rest of the form.

3 Lay in the staircases that slant in the other direction. Place the compass foot on the down DVP bisecting line and draw arcs from the down DVP to create the basic shapes of the staircases. The bottom-most staircase is heading pretty close to straight at the down DVP, so it will be drawn very foreshortened. The arcs from the bull's-eye vanishing points make the staircases line up well.

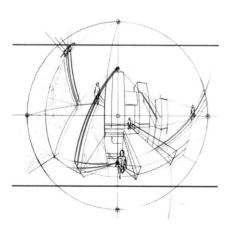

4 Lay in all the bannisters for the stairs. It will take both DVPs, and all five of the bull's-eye vanishing points to trace these bannisters across the image and keep the height correct. Drop your rough figures into the scene, using arcs from the top and bottom vanishing points to make sure you know where vertical is right there.

The figures are all near the bannisters, so use the bannisters to make them properly sized. Draw in the basic shapes of the towers in the distance.

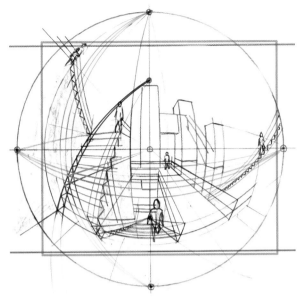

5 Draw the individual stairs in the staircases. The risers of the stairs will be drawn with arcs from the top and bottom VPs, while the platforms of the stairs will be drawn with straight, receding lines pulled to the central vanishing point. Two arcs from the diagonal VPs keep the stairs consistently sized.

Homework

Draw your room (and everything else you can) in five-point perspective. Do a bunch of quick drawings of any space you are in. Use the compass or just wing it, but kick-start your eye into understanding how the system works.

Mystic Kingdom

6 Time to render your scene! Again, keep in mind how your rendering reinforces the volume, form and depth of the piece. The more intense colors go in the foreground, graying out into the distance. The red dress is the strongest red, the mid-ground dragon is a weaker red and the distant dragon is that weak red mixed with the sky blue to help push him back into the distance.

CHAPTER SEVEN

FOUR-POINT PERSPECTIVE

Four-point perspective is

the curvilinear equivalent of two-point perspective. It's an
excellent tool for drawing wide vistas from a very close
point of view, ideal for "letter box" panels in comics. But
maybe more importantly, four-point perspective is very
similar to the perspective of the human eye: a good view
up and down and a huge expanse of vision left and right.

Four-point is also unique in its ability to be adapted into some amazing
tricks including drawing one very wide image: a full 360-degree panorama
or even more.

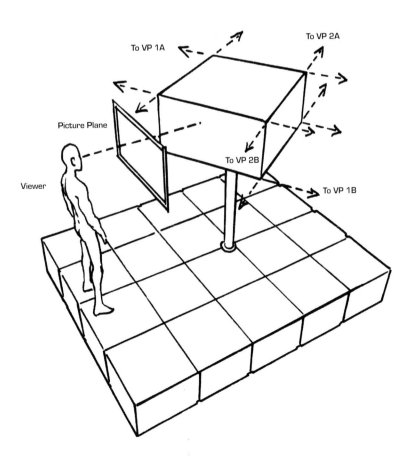

the four-point box

At its most basic, four-point perspective is two vanishing point pairs set overlapping onto a single horizon line, arranged so that all four vanishing points are equally spaced.

As in two-point perspective, in four-point the horizon line should be near the center of the image area. There's more flexibility to nudge the horizon up or down than in two-point, but if you move the horizon to the very top or bottom, or even off the page, you'll create some strange distortions.

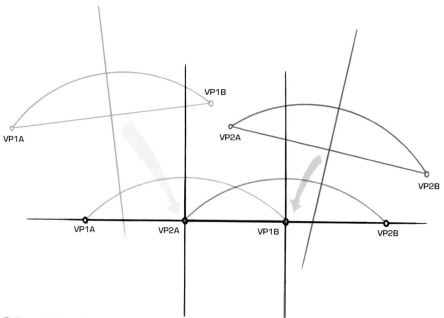

Take It Vertical

Like in two-point perspective, you can turn the four-point world on end. Flip the horizon up vertically to draw great vistas of tall narrow spaces, like a skyscraper and the park in front of it.

↻ Four-Point Framework

To draw the four-point framework, start with a long horizon line. Place four vanishing points equally spaced along the horizon. Draw vertical bisecting lines through the center two vanishing points. It's very important that these lines be exactly 90 degrees to the horizon. If they aren't, you'll be drawing arcs that can only meet one vanishing point of the pair.

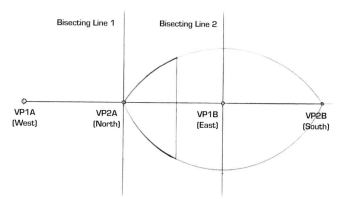

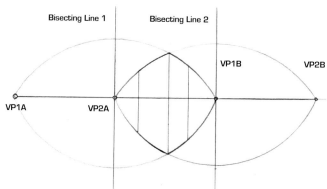

1 Draw the framework as shown on this page. From your framework, draw two arcs connecting the right-hand vanishing point pair, one above the horizon and one below (place the compass point on bisecting line 2 and draw an arc connecting VP2A and VP2B). Somewhere between the two bisecting lines, draw a vertical line that connects the two arcs. This line will be the nearest edge of the box.

2 From the intersection of the vertical line and the two arcs, draw two new arcs—this time between the left-hand vanishing point pair (compass foot on bisecting line 1, connecting VP1A and VP1B). Draw two new vertical lines to represent the outer edges of the box. (Keep these vertical lines between the bisecting lines for now.)

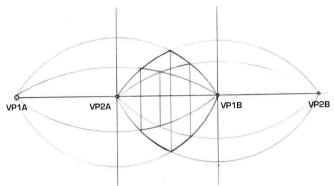

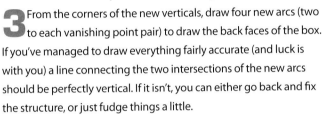

VP1A   VP2A   VP1B   VP2B

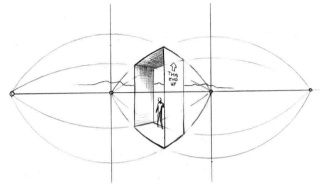

3 From the corners of the new verticals, draw four new arcs (two to each vanishing point pair) to draw the back faces of the box. If you've managed to draw everything fairly accurate (and luck is with you) a line connecting the two intersections of the new arcs should be perfectly vertical. If it isn't, you can either go back and fix the structure, or just fudge things a little.

4 Your structure in is now place. Do any cleanup and rendering your box needs to exist in space.

⊃ *Drawing Larger Arcs*

Drawing the larger arcs is easily done. Like the smaller arcs, the large arcs are drawn with the point of the compass on the bisecting line and the drawing tip rotating between vanishing points. For the smaller arcs (for example, the blue arc) the compass point is on the opposite side of the horizon from the arc it is drawing. For the larger arcs (such as the red and orange arcs), the compass point is on the same side of the horizon as the arc it's drawing.

For arcs very close to the horizon line, your compass won't be able to reach far enough to do the job. You'll need to freehand it, or use a French curve or flexible curve.

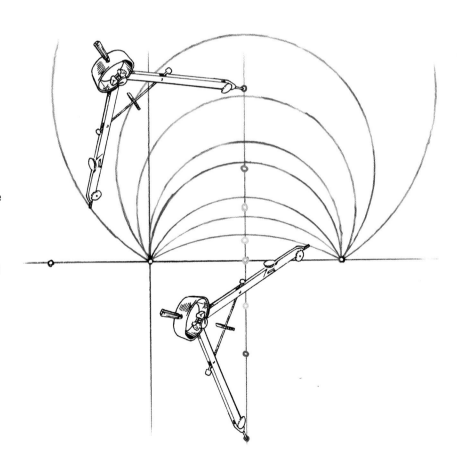

coming out from between bisecting lines

The four-point box is nice and easy for drawings that stay between the bisecting lines, but that's a pretty limited field of view. OK, so it's 90 degrees, which is a wider field of view than you can coax out of straight-line perspective, but you want more than that for the extra work of drawing in curvilinear perspective. Once you've gone past the confines of the bisecting lines, your field of view can stretch way out—120 degrees, 180 degrees, even more.

The first way to spread out beyond the bisecting lines is to draw bigger arcs that stretch out beyond the bisecting lines before arcing back around to the other vanishing point as shown on page 87.

These large arcs extend past the vanishing point pairs to produce graceful and flowing drawings, but drawing with them can sometimes be less than graceful.

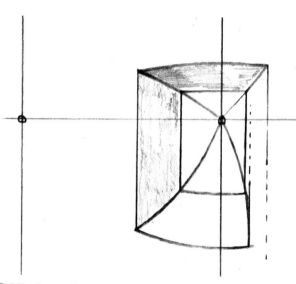

⋂ Missing a Corner
This box, one face of which is drawn with large arcs, has a serious problem. The last vertical edge of the box can't be drawn because the corners won't match. But there are a couple of ways to fix this.

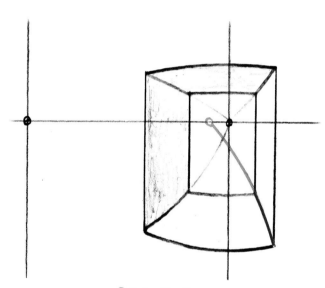

⋂ Fake the Arc
The simplest fix is usually to just fake one of the arcs. Pull the vertical edge from the corner you like best (in this case, down from the top corner to the bottom arc of the box). Then using a French curve (or freehand), draw a new arc that connects the corners it needs to, and don't worry that the new arc doesn't recede to the vanishing point.

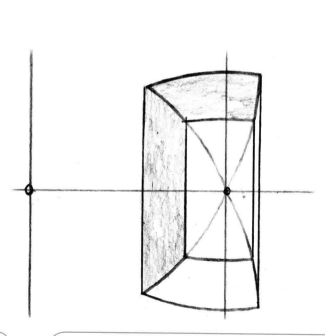

⟳ Create Symmetry
Another solution is to make the box symmetrical across the horizon. If you increase the height of the box (or just move it up) so the verticals of the box are divided in the middle by the horizon, the arcs will all line up properly.

The Strobe Shot

One of the more fun conventions in comic art is the strobe shot—multiple images of the same figure to show the movement over time. This is usually done in two-point perspective, but to create enough space to fit the movement, the camera has to pull way back. But the wide-angle eye of four-point perspective lets you put the viewer right in the middle of the action.

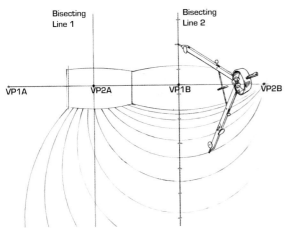

1 Starting from your four-point framework, draw in the basic shapes of two walls of the room. Use the equal ticks dividing trick (page 78) to draw a set of arcs across the floor receding in space. First find the point on the bisecting line that draws the bottom edge of the wall. Mark your equal ticks off from that point and draw the arcs across the room. Move the second vertical corner of the wall to align it with the last arc on the floor so the tiling fits the room nicely.

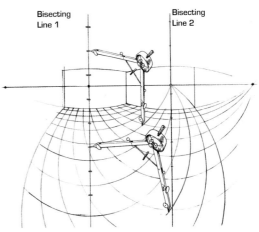

2 Repeat the process for the other direction on the grid. Use the same measurement to space out the ticks on bisecting line 1 that you used on bisecting line 2 in Step 2, and you'll get a nice, square grid.

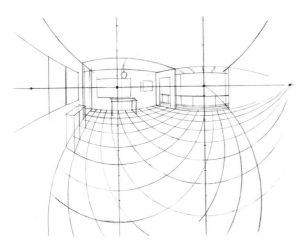

3 Block in the basic shapes of the room: furniture, windows, doors, paintings on the wall—anything that lines up with the main structure of the room.

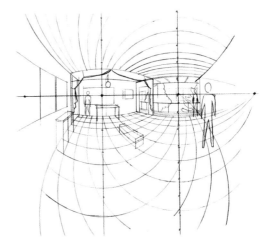

4 As you finish blocking in the shapes in the room (and those visible outside past the porch), you need to prepare for the figures. There will be more than half a dozen in the room, and it's important they all agree with each other and the perspective of the room. The horizon is key for this. Draw the horizon so it will intersect the average-sized man at the top of the shoulders. Rough in a couple of standing figures at some key places in the room to help give a feel for the space. They should be pretty straightforward; the top of the shoulders go at the horizon, the feet go on the floor.

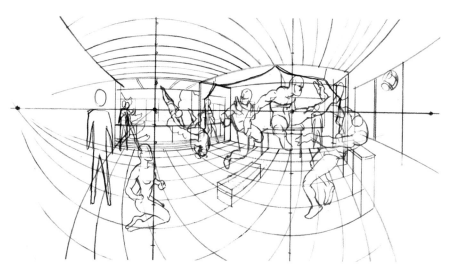

5 Working on an overlay, work out your figures. Ghost simple standing figures anywhere you need some help getting a non-standing figure (kneeling, jumping, whatever) properly sized. For the strobed figures, the trick is to keep them close enough together that you get a nice clear flow between them, but not so tight that they get confused with each other.

Use Mirror Images to Solve Problems

As I was drawing this scene, I realized that my original setup would make the strobe figures read right to left instead of left to right. It was easy to fix this problem. Since I already planned to use a lightbox to do the final drawing, I simply turned the drawing upside down to get its mirror image.

Shaolin vs. Robot

6 Time to take that well-drafted underdrawing and get rendering! Frequently in curvilinear drawings the shapes get broken up so much you can easily freehand the curves or even draw the sections of the curves as straight lines—but that's not quite the case here. For the long, flowing sweeps, you can use a French curve to keep the lines crisp, or even a penholder attached to your compass and voila! Sweeping, dynamic action with the viewer right there in the room with the mayhem.

A distortion-free way to open up beyond the 90-degree confines of the two bisecting lines of the four-point skeleton is to attach more vanishing point pairs to the ends of the original ones—one more on each end, two more, however many you want. This opens up an infinite horizontal extension of your image. It usually doesn't take many. Four or five vanishing point sets can create a full 360-degree view of a scene!

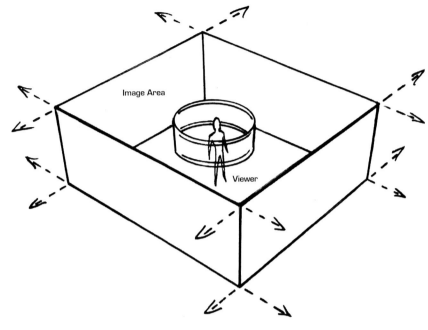

⟳ Establish Vanishing Points

To draw this extended-point version, put as many vanishing points as you want on the horizon, all equally spaced, and draw bisecting lines through them. Each bisecting line will act as the bisecting line for the two vanishing points on either side of the vanishing point the line passes through.

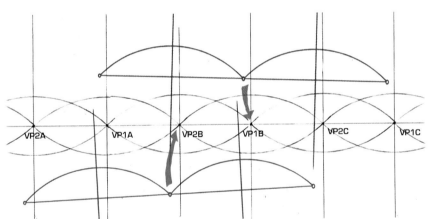

⟳ Filling in the Gaps

The arc farthest from the center that you can draw with this system is a circle with its center on the horizon. Lines on the left side of the bisecting line arc out to meet with the VP two spots to the left, lines on the other side arc out to meet with the VP two spots to the right. But once you get the compass point to the horizon, you can't draw any farther. So where you need to, freehand or use the French curve to drop in a few lines radiating between the two semicircles, meeting the straight bisecting line in the middle.

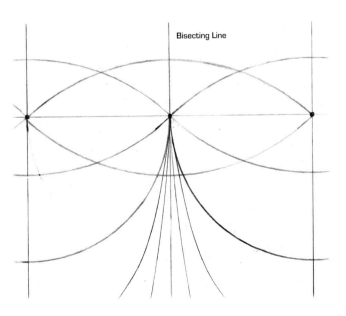

Infinite-Point-Perspective Street Scene

You want an open view that shows an empty street corner. How much of the corner? All of it! So use the infinite-point perspective.

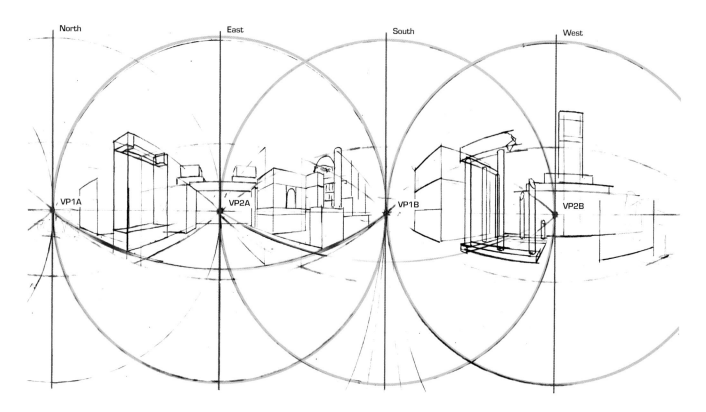

1. Lay out your framework by drawing your horizon. Set your compass to draw a circle the full height of your image. Place the point on the horizon line and draw your circle. Where the circle crosses the horizon line, draw another circle with the compass at the same setting. Draw vertical bisecting lines through each intersection. In this case, align the drawing with the cardinal directions, so vanishing point 1A is north and so on. Rough in the basic shapes of the buildings in the scene.

Things to Keep in Mind

- Technically, the top of the great circles that connect the vanishing point pairs represent up, and the bottom of the circles represent down, so the drawing shouldn't really extend above or below them.

- If you placed new sets of vanishing point pairs halfway between the existing ones, you'd get diagonal vanishing points.

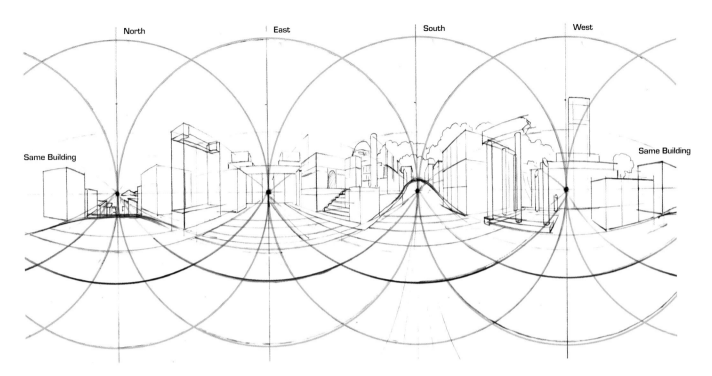

2 To create a bit of visual interest, you don't want the city completely flat. It's a seafront town, and you want to see up into the hills and down to the waterfront. So two of the streets opposite each other will slope. Using the buildings to help you freehand it properly, draw the streets sloping down to the waterfront in the north, and up to the hills in the south. The street will be paved with rough stone, but to help make them recede in size, use the equal-ticks trick to draw a large grid on the ground (don't worry about the parts where the ground is sloping).

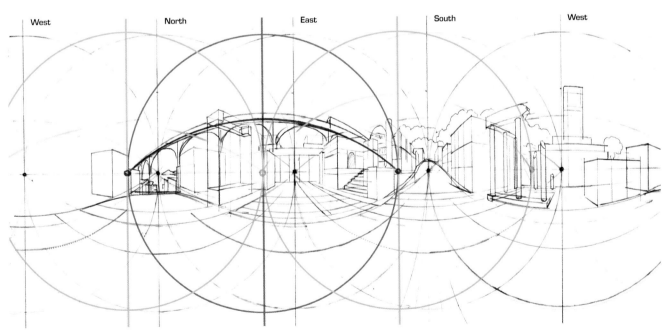

3 There's a large aqueduct passing through the town, and it will be boring if it is lined up with the rest of the buildings. So take a couple new vanishing point pairs and drop them onto the horizon line. It doesn't matter where they go on the line, as long as the distance between the pairs is the same as it is for the other vanishing point pairs. Using the new VP pairs, draw in the main arc of the aqueduct, and then some cross lines to help see how it turns in space.

∩ *Empty Street*

Render your scene! You can show however much of it you want. In this case I've chosen to place the distinctive clock tower at both ends of the piece to reinforce its full turnaround feeling. If you like, you can draw this scene on a huge roll of paper, turn it into a cylinder, and stand in the middle of it, looking all around.

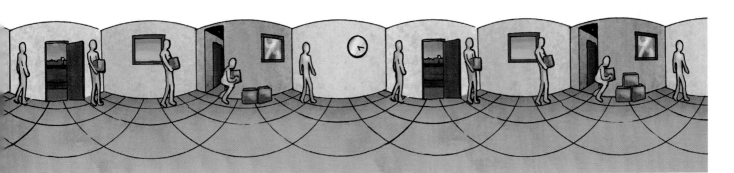

⚙ *Repeating Walls*

So that's four-point perspective. I hope it's opened up a whole new world for you, so to speak. You can extend the four-point perspective as far as you want, although it means you'll be seeing the same walls over and over as you go . . . which in some cases might be kind of neat.

CHAPTER EIGHT

PUTTING IT ALL TOGETHER

Now you've got the tools of

perspective at your disposal, but there are a couple of questions you need to answer about any scene before you can draw it. You know how to use the horizon line, and how to use the vanishing points, but where do you put that line and those points so you can use them?

Most people are just set loose at this point to discover these things by trial and error. You draw your laboratory room, and realize when you go to put people in it they just won't fit, and you have to start over. Or the building you thought you were drawing from a great angle turns out to hide the doorway that's pivotal to the story, and you have to start over. Or the bloody car just won't sit on the street right, no matter how many times you start over. Trial and error involves *a lot* of redoing things.

But the knowledge gained from trial and error isn't some sort of intuitive magic, it's information that can be gathered into concrete lessons to be learned. For example, moving the horizon line upwards is the same as tilting the "camera" downwards. Sliding the vanishing points around changes the angle from which we see the objects we're drawing. So let's set those lessons out in the open and take a look at them. You can borrow a few of my trial-and-error years as your own and get a head start on the process.

Once you've got these last few how-to-get-started lessons under your belt, we'll take the whole perspective-drawing toolbox out and see what we can build with it, start to finish. We'll explore how to choose the best camera angle (and therefore perspective system) to tell the story, and then tackle the nuts and bolts of wrangling together an image that does all those dozens of things we need it to.

Where do you place the horizon? High, low, above the picture, below it? This is probably the most important question of any perspective drawing.

In one-point, two-point, four-point, and five-point, there's a pretty easy answer—it goes more or less in the middle of the drawing. There's some wiggle room (especially in the curvilinear drawings). The horizon can go high or low. High if we're looking a bit down on things, low if we're looking a bit up.

But if it goes too far from the center, you should really be using a different perspective system. If your one-point perspective's horizon goes too high or low, you should use two-point with the horizon line turned vertically. If the horizon in your two-point perspective goes too high or low, you should be using three-point. And if the horizon in your four- or five-point illustration goes too high, you really ought to be using (gasp) six-point perspective where the horizon becomes a circle instead of a line, and two of the three vanishing point pairs rest on it.

In three-point perspective, the horizon line usu-ally goes outside the image area. When the horizon passes through the image area in three-point per-spective, it needs to do so fairly close to the edge of the image, and the third vanishing point needs to be a great distance from the horizon.

Tilting the Camera

Sometimes you can give a perspective illustration some extra punch by rotating the image area a bit. Nothing in the drawing itself changes, but now you're seeing it through a tilted camera. The horizon goes at an angle instead of straight across. (This is called a Dutch angle in film.) This can easily be overdone, though, and hit a comedic rather than a dramatic tone.

What's most famous for those tilted camera shots? The old Adam West *Batman* TV show from the 1960s. If that's not the mood you're trying to evoke, be a little wary.

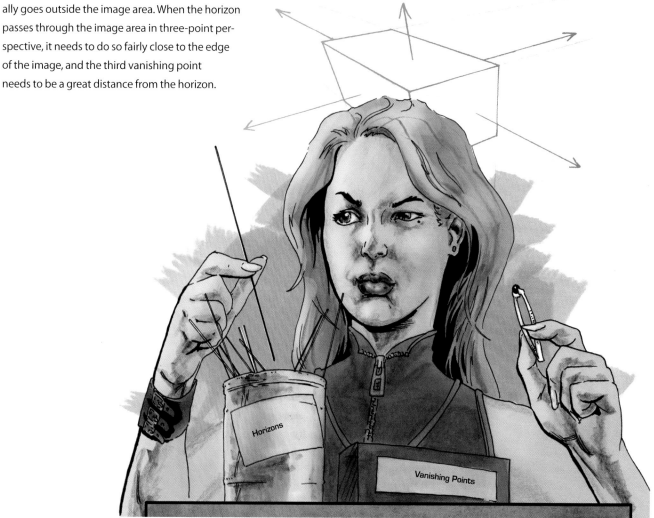

One-Point Perspective

In one-point perspective, the vanishing point goes pretty much in the center of the image. It can wander a bit, but things get distorted if it moves too close to the sides. Sometimes this distortion is pretty unnoticeable, and in the early Renaissance, when one-point perspective was all they knew, it was pretty common to see the vanishing point way over to one side in order to make the receding lines all point towards the most important figure's head. Technically, it should have been done as a two-point drawing, but it looks OK anyway. These days, it can be a bit harder to get away with.

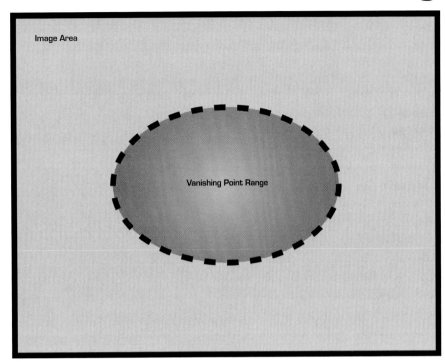

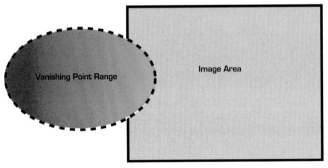

Two-Point Perspective

In two-point perspective, both vanishing points are usually off the edge of the image area, one on each side. If they're equally spaced on each side (red), the viewer is looking at the scene from a 45-degree angle. As one vanishing point moves closer to the center of the image, the other moves farther away (blue). And it's not a 1-inch (25mm) to 1-inch (25mm) movement. Shifting one vanishing point one inch (25mm) closer could move the other vanishing point several inches farther out. As one vanishing point creeps to the edge of the image, even into it, the other gets quite far away. Move it far enough toward the center and the second vanishing point moves an infinite distance away, and you're back at one-point perspective.

Also, remember that the farther apart the vanishing points are from each other, the farther back the viewer seems to be, and the less perspective distortion there is in the image. The closer together the vanishing points are, the closer the viewer seems to be and the more perspective distortion crops up.

Three-Point Perspective

Three-point perspective has the same dynamic as two-point, but with another axis of movement. In addition to the left and right shifts of the two vanishing points on the horizon, you have the same balancing act between the horizon itself and the third vanishing point. Unless you're tilting the camera (Dutch angle), the third vanishing point is centered above the image area. If the horizon and the vanishing points on it are a good distance away from the image area, the third vanishing point can be quite close to the image area, even actually in it.

If the horizon moves close to the image area, or even into it, the third vanishing point moves quite far away (green). Deciding whether the horizon or the third vanishing point should be closer to the center is simply a matter of picturing your scene and deciding if you're going to be looking more up (or down) or more across. If you're looking more up/down than across, the third vanishing point will be closer; if you're looking more across than up or down, the horizon will be closer.

If you want to check that you've got the vanishing points placed properly, find the center of vision (see page 46). If the center of vision falls near the center of the image area, you're golden. If it falls outside the image area, you might want to keep tweaking things.

Again, the farther away from each other the vanishing points are, the farther back the viewer seems to be and the less perspective distortion there is. The closer together they are the closer the viewer seems to be and the more perspective distortion there is.

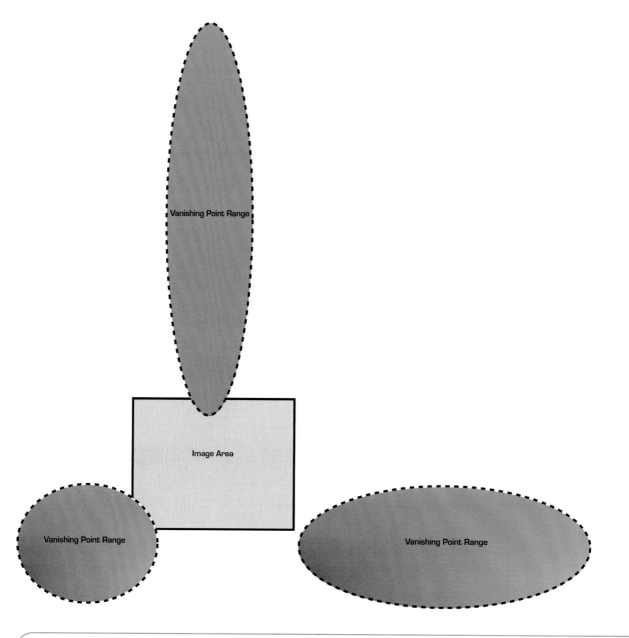

In five-point and four-point curvilinear perspective, there is such a distinct structure to placing the vanishing points that it is more useful to look at where to place the image area within the structure than where to place the vanishing points in relation to the image area.

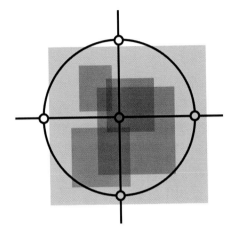

Five-Point Perspective

The field's pretty open as to where you want to put your image area. The larger the image area, the more curve the lines will have; the smaller, the straighter they will seem. So take a pick based on what feel you're looking for. You can go so far out you've got all five vanishing points, or so far in you've kind of wasted your time and should have just been drawing in one-point.

Usually, the central vanishing point will be near the center of the image area, but that's not a hard-and-fast rule. You can even set your image area so that not a single one of the vanishing points is inside. Though, placing the image area so that the central VP is outside but another is inside often looks wonky.

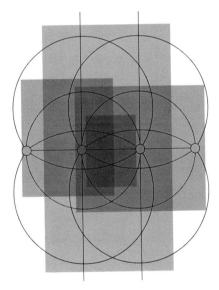

Four-Point Perspective

For four-point perspective, the horizon line must fall inside your image area. Usually pretty near the middle, but not always. The main choice is how wide you want the image to be. You can have no VPs on the page (image area all falls in between the two bisecting lines), one vanishing point, two, three or even four. Usually two or three is sufficient; it starts to look a bit weird once you get up to three vanishing points in the image area. The *Shaolin vs. Robot* illustration (pages 89–90) has two vanishing points on the image area, with a third just barely off and the fourth way off, and that's about as far out as I like to take it, which is pretty far, actually, a little over 180-degree field of vision.

Four-Point Extended Perspective

Horizontally, there's no limit to how far you want to take this kind of drawing; it's just a matter of how far around you want to see. Vertically, the horizon should be within the image area, preferably not too far from the center (though there's more room for shifting than there is in two-point perspective). The image area probably shouldn't extend above or below the great circles that connect the vanishing point pairs.

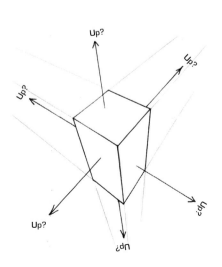

Perspective Doesn't Know Which Way Is Up

Sometimes the question about where to place the horizon is a trick question, because the horizon of the drawing isn't always the horizon of what's being drawn. For example, if you're doing a one-point drawing looking straight down a mine shaft, the real horizon is meaningless to the drawing, but the horizon line of the perspective drawing will be one of the major axes of the mine shaft.

So remember that even though we tend to talk about how these perspective systems are normally used, the same arrangement of vanishing points can be used to draw a scene up, down, forward, backward, left or right.

finding vanishing points from objects

Sometimes the best way to place vanishing points is to start with a drawing of the main object in the scene (or even a few objects) and use the alignments of that object to figure out the best places for the vanishing points.

1 Draw your scene. Don't worry about being too accurate or too pretty, just place the information that you need and keep your mind focused on what the best angle to see it from is, not on how to draw it "right."

2 Find the main lines of your shapes, and pull trial receding lines back from them. These *won't* line up in tidy little vanishing points—don't worry about it.

3 Average in where the trial receding lines meet up, and then take a stab at placing the horizon. In this case not too high. Although you're looking down on the scene, you don't want to be too high above it. Again looking at the averages of where the receding lines meet, make a judgement call and place the vanishing points onto the horizon. The third vanishing point falls far below the image area. For comparison, I have drawn new receding lines to these vanishing points.

4 Use the new vanishing points to re-draw your scene.

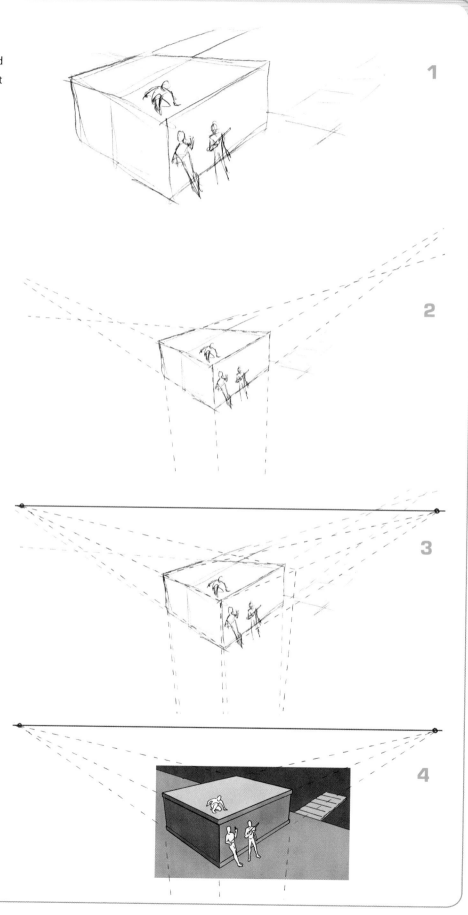

1 If your drawing is something that doesn't have many straight lines to it, the process still works. Again, don't worry about being accurate or pretty. Draw the information that you need, and focus on finding the best angle to see it from.

2 Find the symmetrical points in your shapes and pull trial receding lines back from them. Or eyeball where a straight line would pass through a form and pull that line back. Again, don't expect the lines to converge nicely.

3 Technically, this should be a three-point drawing since we're looking so far down on the ship. But since there aren't any significant verticals to the ship, don't bother with the third vanishing point. Save yourself some time and treat it as a two-point drawing.

Use the average of where the receding lines meet to ballpark how high the horizon should be (in space there's no horizon, but the drawing of a spaceship still has a horizon line). Place the vanishing points where you think they should be. Want the ship to loom up close? Make the vanishing points kind of close in. Want the ship to not have much perspective distortion? Make the vanishing points kind of far apart.

4 Use the new vanishing points to re-draw your ship. You can use doubling space tricks to ensure the symmetry of the ship (see page 68), or you can just wing it!

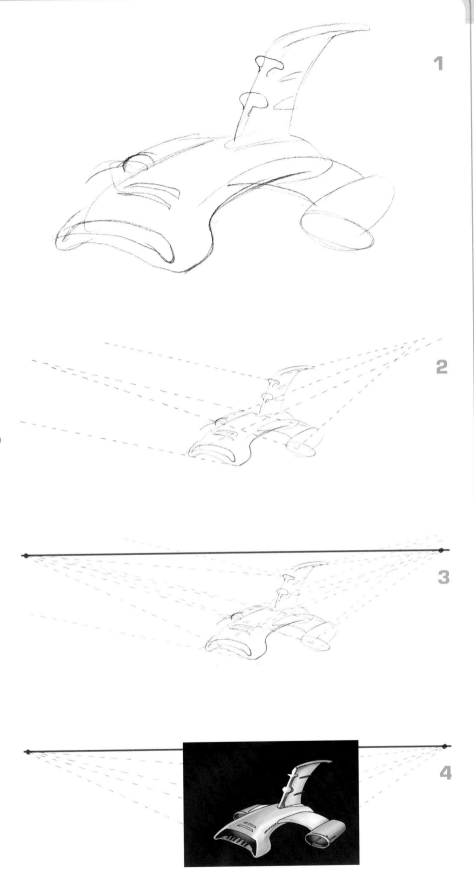

Using Floor Plans and Elevations

Sometimes we use funky perspectives just to shake things up, sometimes we do it to heighten dramatic tension. But sometimes we do it because there's no other way to fit the information we need into a single panel.

Say for instance the script calls for a superheroine lurking in the rafters above a boxing match. One boxer is down for the count, the other is standing over him, the ref is counting, and the victorious boxer's coach is looking through the ropes all smug and self-satisfied. All of this while our sneaky heroine spies on them, gathering clues about the fight-fixing ring. That's a hefty chunk of information to fit into one panel, but we can do it.

Know what the finished panel should look like? Me neither. It's time to start thinking with your pencil.

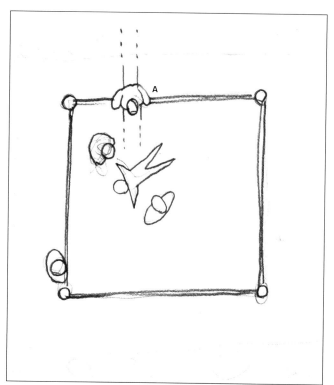

1 Start out by sketching the information you know. This isn't a thumbnail for the panel, it's a floor plan. It lays out what you know, and only needs to be detailed enough to take you to the next stage. In this floor plan, there's no perspective or foreshortening. The heroine in the rafters (labeled A in the drawing) is drawn the same size as the boxers below. Nothing has to be "right" here; you can fix anything later.

2 Don't lose momentum. Next, you need an elevation. An elevation is a side view that, like the floor plan, has no perspective or foreshortening. Kind of like blueprints.

Again, you don't need detail, and you don't need everything to be right—you just need enough information to move on to the next stage.

There really are three elements in this panel: the three people in the ring, the coach outside the ring and our heroine far above the ring. For a single shot to catch all that, the camera needs to either be pulled way back in an extreme longshot, or it needs to be placed on or near a line that passes through all three of our elements.

The elevation in Step 2 doesn't quite work for that, so let's think a few things through. The camera could look up past the coach, past the people in the ring, way up into the rafters to the heroine, but she will be awfully small and hard to see in the rafters. Plus. as this is her point of view in the story, the viewer should try to share it. Let's put the camera behind the heroine, looking down past her to the ring below. In the ring, the view needs to see the coach's face, so he'll have to be somewhere on the opposite side of the ring from the heroine (and more importantly, the camera). Everyone else only requires enough body language to show what they're doing.

3 Draw another elevation, trying to get the camera near a line that runs through the coach, boxers and heroine. If the camera pointed down from the heroine on that first elevation, it would be a straight-down view on the people in the ring, which isn't that interesting. Move the heroine over to the side to allow the camera to look at the action from an angle. Swap the referee and the victorious boxer, so the coach is closer to the champ in the panel, emphasizing their connection.

4 Now lay in a camera, and draw some lines radiating from it. These lines help ballpark the field of view (the edges of the panel. They also help make relative sizes and angles correct. Two lines that frame our heroine's head take up half the ring by the time they get there. This shows her head will be half the size of the ring. And a line going from the camera passes through the standing boxer at about a 45-degree angle—that's handy to know, because that's the angle the viewer will see him at.

So take a stab, using the information you've pulled together in the elevation sketch. You don't need to follow positions slavishly. You can slide things around side to side and still benefit from your earlier work.

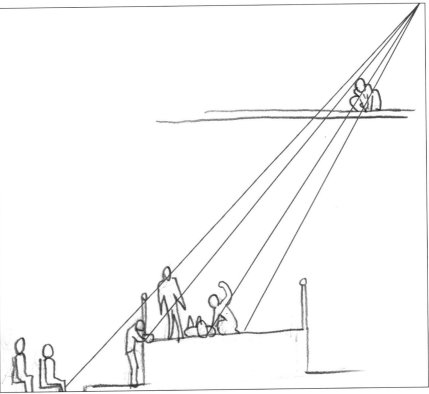

5 OK, so you've got a possible layout. Throw in a spotlight next to the heroine, and enough of a gangplank/catwalk in there so the readers know where she is and that she isn't just floating in space. But what if you wanted to see more of her figure? Just pull the camera back on the elevation.

6 Now the camera lines show the heroine to be a little less than twice the apparent size of the boxers—which makes sense, since she's a little less than twice as close to the camera as they are.

7 Draw another layout to test this arrangement. It's nice enough, but the first layout with the camera closer to the heroine is probably better. This panel isn't about how cool and sexy the heroine is, it's about what's happening in the ring. Go back to the first layout, move the characters around a bit and start to work out vanishing points.

This is three-point perspective—everything converges. The toughest point to place will probably be the vanishing point representing down, but you've got a head start on that.

8 If you look at the elevation, the down vanishing point will be directly below the camera. And the horizon line will be directly to its left. With this information, you can place the down vanishing point and the horizon line in such a way that the perspective within the panel won't be distorted.

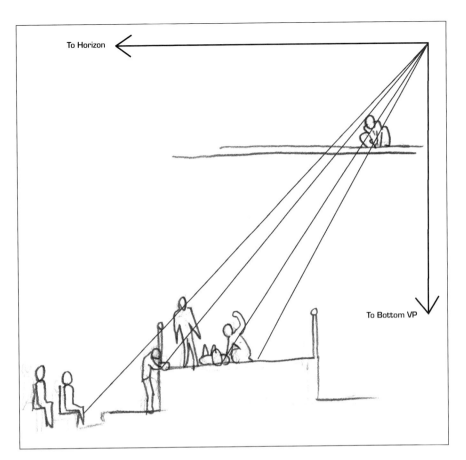

To Horizon

To Bottom VP

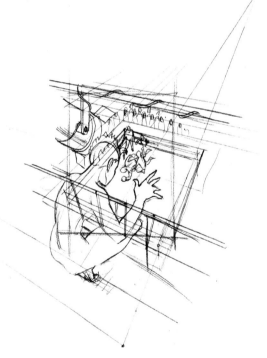

9 After the down vanishing point and the horizon are placed (which can be done on the original drawing, on a tracing paper overlay or on a lightbox to make changes easier), find an object near the center of the panel to work out the final two vanishing points. In this case, the object is the ring.

Draw lines through the middle of the ring, heading towards the horizon. Where these lines cross the horizon are the vanishing points. Remember, these points represent 90 degrees from each other; if the one on the left is west, the one on the right will be north. Draw some test lines for the ring, and make sure you're happy with the vanishing point placement. Once you are, lay in the ring, the ropes, the catwalk and a basic grid for the audience so their chairs line up.

10 To keep the figures in perspective, draw some boxes where the figures are standing. They don't need to mimic the postures of the figures; they're just there to help keep the figures relating to the ground plane and keeping the right way up when you draw them.

There are a couple of elements in the drawing that are rotated so you can't use the same vanishing points. For the KO'd boxer, lay in a box on the floor using two new vanishing points, and for the vanes on the spotlight use another vanishing point. Since all these lines are horizontal, all their vanishing points lie on the horizon.

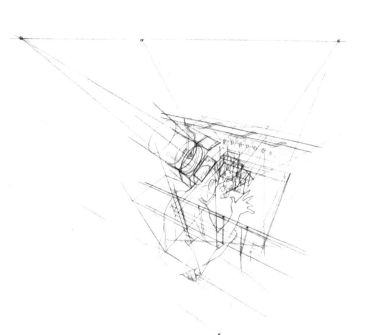

11 Now pause to take stock. The original layout sketch was pretty accurate, but you can see places where the perspective was wrong—the vertical bars in the catwalk especially, as well as the heroine figure and the vertical supports on the spotlight. But changing these things to fit the perspective isn't going to affect the composition, so you're ready to go. Now you can fly through drawing the finished panel, because the perspective layout has solved the major problems.

Spying From the Rafters

Using Thumbnails to Find Perspective

This illustration shows a wall-climbing hero as he tries to keep tabs on a trio of jet-pack villains wreaking wanton destruction about the city. It's a bit of an establishing shot, with a lot of information to pack into it. You need to see enough of the city to get an idea of the destruction, but be in tight enough to see the lone hero stuck to the side of a building. You could settle for a shot from behind the hero to look over his shoulder at his point of view, but it is nicer to include his face in the shot.

1 Create a rough sketch to start from. This sketch has the elements, and an exploding building in the foreground, but maybe that building in the foreground forces all the figures to be a little smaller than you'd like.

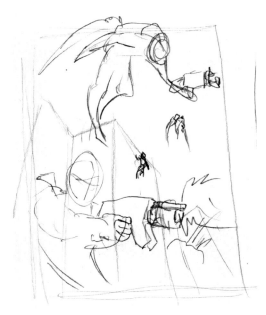

2 The second sketch is a bit better, it's got the marauders up front, nice and scary. And the sky in the background gives the scene a bit of breathing room. But the hero is still pretty small—forget seeing any facial expression on him.

3 The third sketch diplays the hero fairly large in size and gives a good view of the destruction he's surveying. But the villains are a bit small. You could put a bad guy in the foreground, but you'll still see the hero from the back, and there's only so much body language you can create with a guy stuck to a wall.

4 The fourth sketch has some potential. It's hard to show the hero largeish without the building getting huge in the picture and blotting everything out, but there are some tricks you can use.

You can blow off part of the building. Then it can serve double duty in showing the wanton destruction *and* setting up the challenge of chasing flying foes when the hero can't fly himself. It also can create a pretty good composition with the strong diagonal coming up through the bottom villain, and the opposite strong diagonal passing through the hero and the other two villains.

Once the thumbnail is finished, it's time to lay out the perspective. The way the viewer is looking up at that building calls for three-point perspective. The viewer is looking more across at the building than up the building. The horizon will be closer to the image area than the top vanishing point, but the viewer is still looking up enough that the horizon will be below the image area.

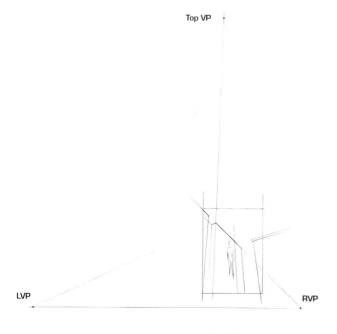

5 These vanishing points draw a building but not the one we need. When you sketch in a figure about the size you want the hero to be, you see that the section of the building he's climbing would only be about 9 feet (3m) across, and multistory buildings just aren't built that way. So you need to slide the image area to the right to place the face of the building at a more extreme angle. The top vanishing point should move along with the building.

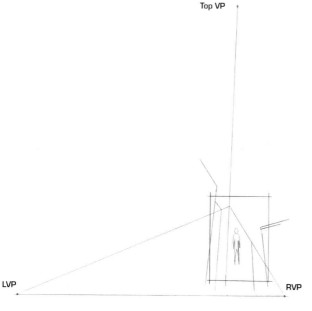

6 This setup is better. The building has enough facade to allow detail, but it's angled enough that you can put a decent-sized figure climbing on it without the building looking tiny or taking up the whole image area.

7 Find all three diagonal vanishing points on the three-point triangle (see pages 46-47). You may not need all three but it's best to be overprepared. Draw in a standing figure floating next to the side of the building to help establish story height. Use the diagonal vanishing point between the right and top vanishing points to divide up the face of the building into a 2" × 2" (5cm × 5cm) grid. Each square will represent about 8' × 8' (2.5m × 2.5m). Move the right side of the building a bit if it helps make things come out evenly. Divide two more verticals onto the grid. (Now you've got top-to-bottom divisions of two 8-foot (2.5m) stories, and side-to-side divisions of four 4-foot (1.25m) sections.

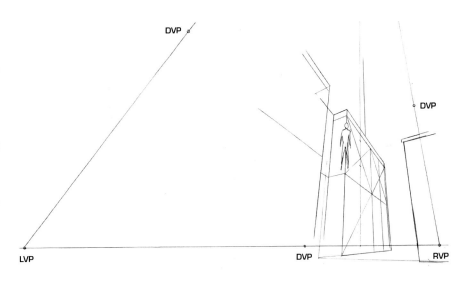

8 Draw out the structures of the building's facade (windows, doors, ornaments) using the divisions to keep things consistently sized. Draw more of the skyscraper above the protrusion that the hero will be climbing and use the diagonal vanishing point between the top and right vanishing points to grid it up. Since the building on the left will be pretty far in the foreground, a good brick finish might look nice on it. Use the diagonal vanishing point between the left and top vanishing points to divide the building up into a smallish grid so you can draw convincing bricks.

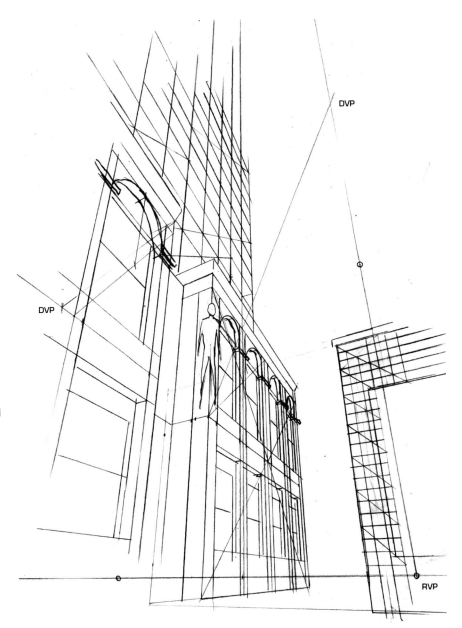

9 Now, stick the hero to the wall. Use the story height and the sketched standing figure to help get his size right. Use all the divisions and shapes you've drawn on the face of the building to help your eye make sure that every hand and foot that should touch the building actually is and not floating out in space above or penetrating inside the building.

Take a step back and look at the pose. His right hand is directly above his right foot, but his left foot is waaaaay across the building facade (almost 4 feet [1.25m] away according to the grid). That makes his balance a little funky, and I'm not sure he could realistically reach that far. You should probably move his right hand or his left foot farther to the middle.

10 Moving the right hand would put it on the glass, and while our hero's a good climber, he's not a housefly. So take a stab at re-drawing the hero with his left foot moved over to the right.

11 Bring in the villains! Flying characters are great to draw. There's a lot of freedom since there's no need to worry about whether the figures agree with the ground plane or not. Also, it allows more slop in terms of scaling the figures. Draw the character a little too big, and it's almost never wrong. He's just a little closer to the camera. Same thing if you draw the flying character a little too small—he's just a bit farther away. Use this freedom to really fine-tune the scene's composition. Note how the rear jet packers' feet point to the hero, and how that same line continues through the hero's posture to point at the face of the villain in the foreground.

Rocket-Pack Peril

12 Time to render! The tight perspective structure you've drawn should make the buildings a snap and take the guesswork out of the bricks on the building on the right. Make sure your color choices reinforce the perspective depth of the scene and the mood. Use your higher-intensity colors in the foreground and get the strongest contrast light-to-dark in the foreground. As the image goes back in space, gray out the intensity, and lower the light-to-dark contrast. *Warm colors advance, cool colors recede* isn't a hard-and-fast rule, but it does work nicely when you use it.

CHAPTER NINE

TRICKS AND TROUBLESHOOTING

Special vanishing points,

X-marks-the-spot, ellipses, diagonal vanishing points, transferring measurements, circles of vision—you've got most every tool of perspective you could need in your tool-box. This chapter is your duct tape and bailing wire.

Sometimes you don't need a fully developed perspective drawing, just the illusion of one. Being a comic book artist means cranking out hundreds of individual drawings. One issue of a comic book might have more individual images than an artist in another field might produce all year. So there are tricks to economize your time—and once your mind's eye has that instinctive grasp of how perspective works, these tricks can do a dandy job.

But it's not just corner cutting we need to do; we need to be able to fix perspective problems in our drawings. We need to recognize distortions from poorly placed vanishing points and know how to fix them, often by just going back to the rules and making it right. But every once in awhile, we can use a little artist's sleight of hand to cover up the problem so that no one can see it.

To round out this chapter, we'll take a closer look at the transition from the structural layout of a perspective draw-ing to the finished image. One of the pit-falls of amateur perspective drawing is an over-reliance on lines drawn by a ruler; this can give the final image (no matter how accurately drawn) a sterile feel and destroy the believability we're working to cre-ate. Put down the ruler. We've got ways of avoiding those pitfalls.

shortcuts and background fakes

Once you've got the fundamentals of perspective drawing under your belt, you can find some shortcuts to effectively fake a perspective drawing into looking believable without laying out a full perspective drawing.

The key in perspective drawing, no matter how faked it is, is the horizon. Sometimes you don't need to pin it down exactly, but you need to know the gist of where it should be before you draw anything in your scene.

Need to draw eighty panels to finish off your current comic book issue? You probably want to cut corners in a few places—and you can quite comfortably get away with it if you don't overuse these cheats. In my opinion, the cheats are never as satisfying as doing things properly, but practicality says we all wind up using these from time to time.

⋒ Vertical Objects

Vertical objects, like street lamp poles and signposts make great shortcut backgrounds. As long as the horizon is in the panel (you're not looking up or down too much), all you need is a few vertical lines and maybe a few texture marks. If you really want to sell the roundness of the pole, draw some bands around it by laying in some rough ellipses. No need to be too accurate about how thick or thin the ellipse is since it doesn't have to agree with much of anything else in the picture. Throw a cast shadow across a wall in the back at most any angle you like and you create a decent feeling of space without having to take the vaguest stab at placing a vanishing point.

⋒ Standing Figures

It's easy to place standing figures together as long as you can run a horizon line through the same point on each figure (in the above example, it's somewhere around the nose or eyes—the characters aren't exactly the same height, and one's a little hunched over, so we're allowed some extra slop before anything looks wrong).

A row of windows (or paintings, or TV screens) creates a sense of place. Angle the line above the horizon up away from it. Angle the line for the bottom of the windows down and away from the horizon. Drop in simple verticals to complete the edges—eyeballing their placement—and you've very quickly indicated a space that would take a full two-point drawing to really render.

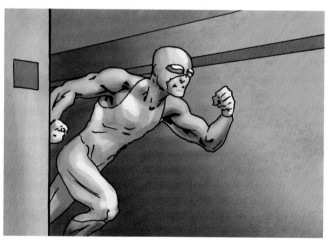

⋒ Walls and Corners

You can take the faked two-point even further by indicating some wall and ceiling corners. A foreground wall is easily done with just a vertical line. Behind that angle some lines away from the horizon (which in this case is nebulously placed somewhere in the lower half of the panel). The top angled line becomes the corner between the ceiling and wall, and others can detail the wall to define the plane of the wall better.

Cement the foreground wall and its angle by angling some new lines opposite to the angles you used for the other wall to fake a rectangle for a control panel, light switch or hanging photo.

⋒ A V-Shaped Edge

Jot in a quick moderate upshot to round out your imposing figure by drawing a wide "V" for the edges where the ceiling meets the walls. Drop a line down from the point of the V for the corner between the walls. You can draw it with a vertical, or angle it away from center slightly to fake a bit of a three-point worm's-eye feel.

Technically, the tiles in the ceiling should increase in angle the farther they get from the horizon, but that's hard to fake accurately. You can find a vanishing point for them or if you're in a real rush just draw them all parallel to one of the wall/ceiling lines. It's not "right," but comic artists get away with it every month.

⋒ Hanging Figures off the Horizon

When your camera is high in the scene but the horizon is still in the panel, you've got a two-point perspective scene. To populate the ground below, you could use a series of vanishing points to project multiple figures off the first, or you can just hang them off the horizon (this shortcut trick is actually solid-gold accurate).

Since the figures are way below the horizon, just stand an invisible person on the head of each of them. The horizon will cut all the invisible people at the same level. If the camera really goes way up there, you can stack two, three, four or however many invisible people on the heads of your figures to reach the horizon. (This works as long as you don't start looking down from the horizon; then you've got a three-point drawing, and this trick doesn't quite work so simply anymore.)

Fake a ground surface for your people to stand in by angling a few lines away from the horizon (if you want planks or tiles, go ahead and use a vanishing point; it'll be worth it). And flying guys? You can draw them wherever you want.

⟳ Perspective in Nature

Perspective is still at work in nature, but there's not the uniformity of size and angles that vanishing points help draw (apart from vertical—nature uses that angle a lot).

Place your horizon line and keep in mind that things look smaller the farther away they are and that atmospheric perspective will make distant objects less distinct and contrasting, and that's all you need to get drawing.

curing distorted elements

Sometimes when you wing it, or just don't place the vanishing points quite right, things come out wrong. No problem. No matter how bad it is or how much you need to change, it's done you some good in figuring out how to draw the scene. Fixing the problem, even if you restart from a completely different angle, will be much easier than starting from scratch.

Moving the Vanishing Point

The most common mistake in perspective drawing is extending the drawing to a cone of vision that is too large. A more useful way to think of this is that you've put the vanishing points in too close.

How Wide Is Too Wide?

How big your cone of vision/field of view can be is somewhat a matter of personal preference. If you're into numbers, most people put it at 60 or 70 degrees (a 60-degree cone of vision means you can see 30 degrees to the left of the line of vision, and 30 degrees to the right).

Sometimes it's a good and dramatic thing to go a little farther than that. Many of the illustrations in this book go well beyond a 60-degree cone and into the "dramatic" realm in order to more clearly show the concepts they're illustrating.

⊘ Distorted Room

Take a look at this room. It looks OK to the left side of the central wall, but the right side—ugh. That orange couch is smooshed into some strange sliding sideways shape, and the red ceiling panel flares so much it doesn't look like it could ever be a rectangle.

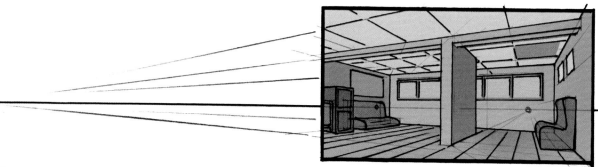

⊘ Corrected Room

To fix the distortion, you only need to move the vanishing points out. It's easiest if you slide that right vanishing point out of the image area, but if the scene really calls for this view, you can still make it work. Slide the vanishing point that's in the image area as far to the side as you can, and move the other vanishing point way out there. The uncomfortable feeling of the room goes away. The couch turns into something that looks like it could actually exist, and that red ceiling tile looks just fine.

Checking the Horizon

Another common problem is that the space is drawn OK, but things fall apart when characters get dropped into the scene.

Horizon

Horizon

⋒ *Distorted Characters*

Check out where the horizon falls for the architecture (a nice, simple, one-point perspective drawing). The horizon cuts the figures in the distance through the neck, but goes way over the heads of the figures in front, even though they're all supposed to be standing on the same level.

⋒ *Corrected Characters*

To fix this, all you need to do is get the two elements in agreement with the same horizon. We could re-draw the foreground figures, but then they'd have to go above the horizon and they'd cover up the background figures. So move the horizon up a little bit and re-draw the room, now with all the figures falling below the horizon.

The wall on the left makes a handy point to measure figure height from. The bottom corner with the floor obviously has to be bottom-of-foot height, and that stripe running down the wall is at neck/shoulder height.

curing full-scene distortion

Maybe you've drawn a panel that isn't awful, but it's off enough that it just feels wrong—and certainly off enough that an editor would jump on it as an example of why he or she shouldn't hire you.

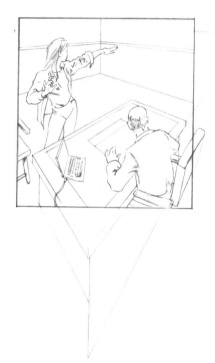

1

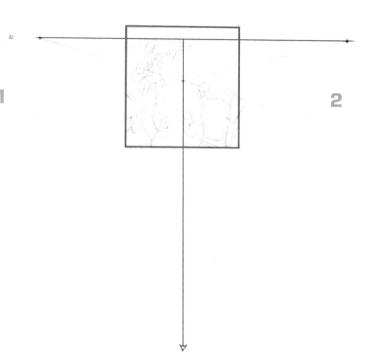

2

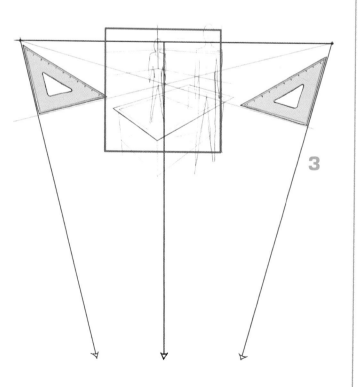

3

1 The main problem with this panel is the desk. Its shape distorts and makes it hard for the people around it to exist in space. It's not as severe as the two-point room with the orange couch, but it's bad enough. Take a look at the vanishing points. It's obvious that they're in too close, and the horizon is awfully high. If you want to keep it up there, the drawing should be done in three-point perspective instead of two-point.

2 Extend the horizon and place the VPs farther out. This scene needs to be converted to three-point, so you need to find the bottom vanishing point. Mark the center of vision right in the center of the panel. Drop a vertical line through that point. The bottom VP will be somewhere on that line. To start figuring out where, draw two more lines, one from each vanishing point, that pass through the center of vision and continue on.

3 The lines that connect the two vanishing points on the horizon to the bottom vanishing point will cross the lines that pass through the center of vision at right angles. Use your triangle to find and draw lines that are at right angles to the center of vision line and pass through the vanishing points. Both lines will cross the big

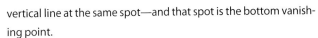

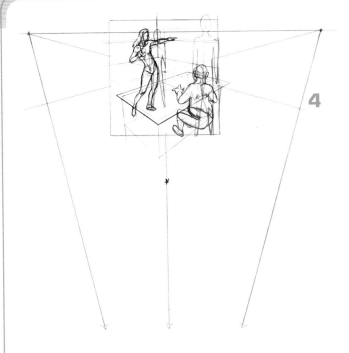

vertical line at the same spot—and that spot is the bottom vanishing point.

Now that you've got all three vanishing points, re-draw the desk, the walls and the ghost in two standing figures (the man is much taller than the girl, so you can make his ghost bigger if you want).

4 Draw the figures into the scene. To cement them to the perspective of the ground plane, start with their "footprints." For the standing girl, this is literally her footprint, the outline of her shoes on the floor. For the seated man, the footprints are his feet and the outline of his buttocks and thighs against the plane of the chair's seat.

5 To avoid any sloppiness, find the magic spot on the vertical line through the center of vision. Use the magic spot to locate the vanishing point pairs to draw the computer and the chair the girl has just risen from (remember, the chair's seat will be as high as her knees).

6 Render the scene and enjoy the improvement!

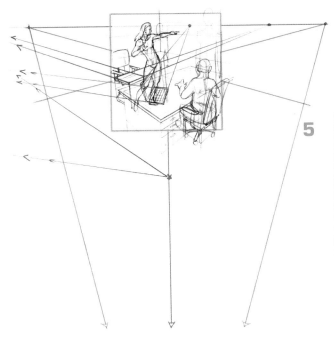

tricks and cheats

I feel a little guilty including this section in this book. Obviously, it's better to get things right, but there are also a couple of ways to cover up distortion problems. They don't actually fix the problem, and aren't technically right, but they do the job of creating a drawing that looks and feels right. And at the end of the day, isn't that the idea?

Composite Perspective

All objects facing the same direction *should* converge to the same vanishing points, but we can sometimes cheat this rule to open up our cone of vision and show a little more than we could get away with if we did things right.

1 You want a vanishing point well towards the middle of the page (maybe compositionally that's really where you want the end of the street, or whatever you're drawing, to be), but you don't want the flat-on feel of one-point perspective. Placing one side of the street to a set of vanishing points draws them just fine, but will severely distort anything drawn on the other side of the vanishing point (like the red ceiling tile and orange couch on page 118). So only draw the left-hand side of the street.

2 Since the road is the same width its entire distance, the buildings should be parallel, and they should converge at the same vanishing point as their partners across the street. They *should*, but we're breaking some rules here. Slide a new vanishing point a little more toward the center and draw the second set of buildings as a one-point perspective drawing.

3 It's the space that falls between these two sets of buildings that's the trick. Draw a new set of vanishing points that splits the difference between the two you've already got. The right vanishing point is between the previous two, and the left vanishing point is well past the first left vanishing point. Use this new VP setup to draw the objects that fall between the two rows of houses.

4 Keep track of which vanishing points draw which objects as you refine the drawing. Take a step back and see if the cheat will be seamless or whether it will be obviously wrong to the viewer.

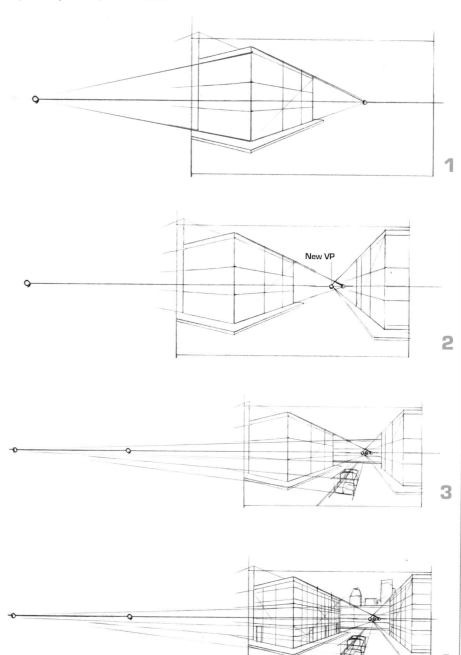

New VP

1

2

3

4

5 Render and enjoy your deception. Unless someone breaks out a ruler to check your vanishing points, no one will ever notice you've bent the rules.

Curvilinear vs. Composite

Curvilinear perspective often does the same job that composite perspective does, and can be more of an elegant solution.

Masking

Sometimes the easiest way to disguise perspective distortion is to cover it up. Place other elements (trees, rocks, figures, capes, clouds, trash, word balloons) over the offending part of the drawing.

⬆ Masking With Background Elements
This is a neat castle, but in the left-hand illustration, look at where those towers meet with the ground plane—it does not look like they're vertical at all. You can re-draw the towers, raise the top VP, lower the horizon, and fix it for real, or maybe you can just cover it up, as is the case in the right-hand illustration. Draw a big boulder, and a bit of greenery to cover up the offending angles. You're left with a good, sweeping, dramatic shot of the castle, but with the wrong-looking bits tastefully covered up.

⬆ Masking With Character Elements
Here's another instance where the vanishing points are too close in and the corners of the image area near the closer vanishing point look a little bad. No problem. Alter the cape to cover the offending distortion, and your scene is saved.

put down that ruler

Sometimes your horizon and vanishing points are all perfectly placed, and the center of vision lines up nicely with the center of the panel, yet things still don't look right because of the way things are drawn. You've got your ruler in hand, and it's easy to succumb to the temptation of eagerly ruling out lines from a vanishing point, only to find you haven't drawn a building, you've drawn a blueprint of a building. It isn't believable. You want to feel like you can open the door and walk right in, but you don't.

⋂ No Depth
Everything is perfectly ruled and placed, but it's not a building. At best it's a blueprint of a building taped to the outside of a giant cardboard box. None of those doors or windows look like they could actually open. If you find yourself drawing each side of a three-point perspective building with only two vanishing points, you're probably falling into this trap.

⋂ Use the Third Vanishing Point
Bringing the third vanishing point into play on every side turns those lines on the building into what they should be—indications of a change in the depth of the building's surface. The change is most notable at the arches, but also look at the windows and the columns between them—they aren't just lines on a flat surface any-more, they're three-dimensional structures. So now it has depth, but it still doesn't feel real. The door is there, but it won't open.

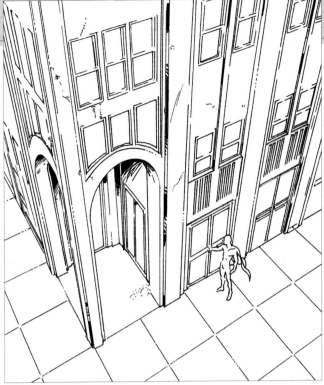

⌒ Lose Some Lines

In real life, the play of light and shadow and wear and tear on the building make it so we don't see all of every line of a building; they get broken up, and our mind fills in the gaps to create the full straight line. Our brain is used to doing this and kind of enjoys it. Break up the long lines in the drawing and let the mind fill them back in, and suddenly the drawing is a lot more engaging and a little more real. But it's still a touch antiseptic.

⌒ Add Texture Marks

Along with the broken lines, and working with them, throw in some texture marks around the building. Use them to reinforce the planes of the shape and show the eye that the building is made of stone or concrete, not smooth plastic.

⌒ Create Personality

From here it's a matter of taste. Some artists will like the slick precision of the last version, while others will feel it's still too perfect and antiseptic to feel like it really exists. Maybe it's OK for a shiny new building, but for an inner-city structure that's decades old, it's a harder sell.

    You need to put down your ruler and draw those straight lines freehand. Use the ruler judiciously here and there to give a hint of the original precision of the structure (how much depends on the situation—more for a shiny, new high-tech medical laboratory, a lot less for a dirty apartment or an old brick building). Give the building a sense of place and a sense of history by giving each line a handmade feel.

For my money, you now have everything you need to know to do top-notch perspective drawings. As soon as you start putting this information into practice, it will become part of you. You'll learn to see better and draw better.

Vanishing points and horizons will soon become second nature, if they aren't already. But you'll probably never remember how to construct a three-point setup from a 90-degree cone of vision, and you don't have to. You've got a reference book (this one!) to show you how to do that anytime you need to (pages 55-57, if you're curious).

One of the special challenges in comic book and fantasy art is you need to be able to draw all this stuff out of your head. Reference material is useful, but you should never chain yourself down to it. You need to be able to draw anything, from any angle, without having the thing in front of you to study (which is why a comic artist needs to know so many more perspective tricks than, say, a landscape painter).

But one of the best ways to build believability into your invented drawings is to practice drawing your real-life world. Do studies of the spaces and objects around you. They don't have to be pretty; they just have to help you teach yourself. Look at the world around you, hold your head still, and point to where the vanishing points would be. Study the vanishing points of drawings and photographs.

And remember, have fun! You're creating entire worlds in those little boxes.

Go draw!

Index

If You're Going To Draw—
Draw With Impact

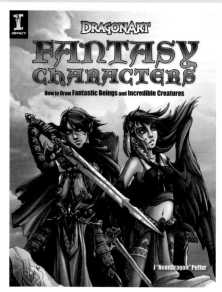

Conjure up your own fantasy realms by pulling inspiration from fairy tales, legends and things that go bump in the night. Color-coded, step-by-step demonstrations show you how to create a sordid cast of creatures, including goblins, orcs, sprites, angels, mermaids, centaurs, vampires, werewolves, banshees and more. Breathe life into your beings by basing them upon fundamental human anatomy—proportions, facial expressions and gender-specific characteristics. Accessorize each being by tailoring them with tusks, wings, hooves, daggers, armor and various apparel, from the fine garb of nobles to peasant rags.

ISBN-13: 978-1-58180-852-0
ISBN-10: 1-58180-852-6
Paperback, 128 pages, #Z0055

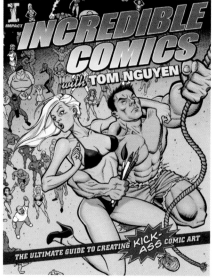

Professional comic book artist Tom Nguyen shows you how to make your work stand out from the cookie-cutter masses. Populate your world with convincing heroes, villains and citizens. Pump-up the drama with perspective, page design and other powerful techniques. Learn to put it all together to tell awesome, action-packed stories! Illustrated with dos, don'ts, and tons of step-by-step instruction, this is a real-world guide to the skills you need to make it as a comic book artist. Armed with these inside secrets and tricks-of-the-trade, you'll be more than just another good artist, but a bona fide, super-hero-style storyteller!

ISBN-13: 978-1-58180-946-6
ISBN-10: 1-58180-946-3
Paperback, 128 pages, #Z0662

If you harbor a love of imagery most foul, of demons and monsters and devils of all sorts … then welcome to the book from hell. Within its pages lurk sadistic orcs, flesh-eating zombies, blood-thirsty dragons, unholy monstrosities and dreaded beasts of legend and lore. If you dare to open this book and unleash such horror, venture forth and learn everything a good monster-maker needs to know including how to spawn a loathsome range of creatures, step by gruesome step in 29 demonstrations. Plus learn tips for making your creatures even creepier with the skillful use of point-of-view, iconic and action poses, color and shadow.

ISBN-13: 978-1-58180-926-8
ISBN-10: 1-58180-926-3
Paperback, 128 pages, #Z0569

Since landing her first professional gig at age 15, superstar cartoonist Colleen Doran has accumulated more than 500 credits to her name as an artist, writer and designer. In this book, she shares the lessons she's learned along the way, giving you a real-world understanding of how to create polished, publishable manga comics and graphic novels just like a pro. Learn how to develop stories in the Japanese manga style versus a traditional Western style of comics; turn your everyday experiences and observations into viable characters and plots; submit a book package to a publisher; and explore alternative publishing options, such as self-publishing, blogs, fanzines and mini-comics. This book will help you tailor classic techniques to suit your own unique style, and guide you toward your creative destiny.

ISBN-13: 978-1-58180-985-5
ISBN-10: 1-58180-985-9
Paperback, 128 pages, #Z0842

These books and other fine IMPACT titles are available at your local fine art retailer, bookstore or from online suppliers or visit our website at www.impact-books.com.